Honour Thy Father

Recollections of Sussex Rural Life
Over Two and a Half Centuries

as recounted
by

Lillian M. Hunt

with additional historical research and notes by
Jennifer F J Goldsmith

2006

Published by

S & J Goldsmith Publications

12 Park Rise, Petworth, West Sussex, GU28 0HU

ISBN 0-9552690-0-8

Printed and bound by RPM Print & Design,
2-3 Spur Road, Quarry Lane, Chichester, West Sussex, PO19 8PR

Acknowledgements

Thanks must go to all those without whose help Lillian Hunt's manuscript would never have been published, particularly Alison McCann and the ever-helpful staff of the West Sussex Record Office in Chichester.

To Joy Peachey, Grace Terry, Alf Scammell, Jonathan Knight and Tony Madgwick for searching out their collections of photographs, letters and family information.

To Joanna Embleton for her wonderful maps and to Frank Penfold and Peter Jerrome for invaluable advice and information on rural life in the Petworth and Arundel areas.

Most importantly to Lillian's daughter Susan, whose determination that her mother's dream be realized has made this book possible.

Finally to RPM Print & Design for their tremendous help in putting together the finished production of this book.

Lillian Mary Hunt nee Elliott age 20.

INTRODUCTION

How many of us regret that we did not listen more closely and note down the stories that our parents and grandparents told us of their lives? There can be few of us who have not at one time or another thought, "oh why didn't I ask about that, and now it is too late."

Lillian Hunt (nee Elliott) need have no regrets on that score; she did the very thing that so many of us regret not having done. She listened, and from an early age, noted down the stories that her father and grandfather told. Stories not just of their own lives and work but stories that they in turn had heard from their own fathers and grandfathers. In writing down these stories Lillian is the chronicler of an oral tradition dating back at least to 1735.

Lillian's family the Elliotts and the Whitingtons, had been Agricultural Labourers in Sussex certainly since the beginning of the 18th Century. Agricultural Labourers may appear in their thousands in the pages of the Census Returns and Parish Registers but they rarely find a voice to tell the real story of their lives. In Lillian Hunt they have that voice. Factual, funny, sad, philosophical and even practical – how did you make Scrap Pie or protect yourself against the Spanish Flu pandemic of 1918? The answers are here in this marvellous account.

When I began reading through the sheaf of foolscap pages Lillian left to her daughter Susan I had no idea what they contained. Working through the pages I have been endlessly fascinated by the picture of a way of life that Lillian paints, a way of life now long gone.

The stories that Lillian recounts had, in the main been handed down through her grandmother's family the Whitington's of Kirdford. Wherever possible I have checked these stories against information in the West Sussex Records Office and others sources. The degree of factual accuracy in Lillian's account is astounding, even when recording events that had occurred 240 years earlier.

Lillian called her account 'Honour Thy Father'. No attempt has been made to alter or edit her words. My task has been merely to carry out research and add additional historical notes. That task has been an endless pleasure.

Jennifer Goldsmith
Chichester
January 2006

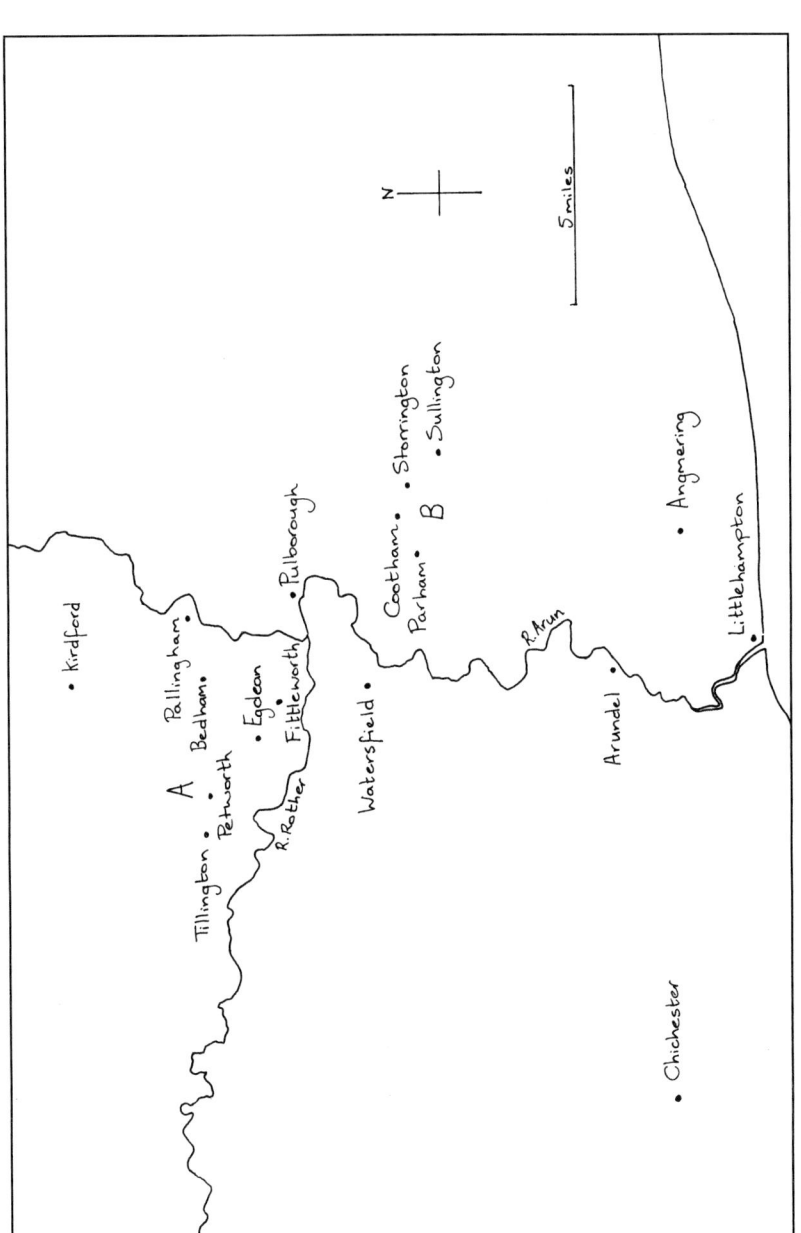

Map 1: Locations of the two families, the Whitingtons and the Elliotts. A = Whitingtons   B = Elliotts

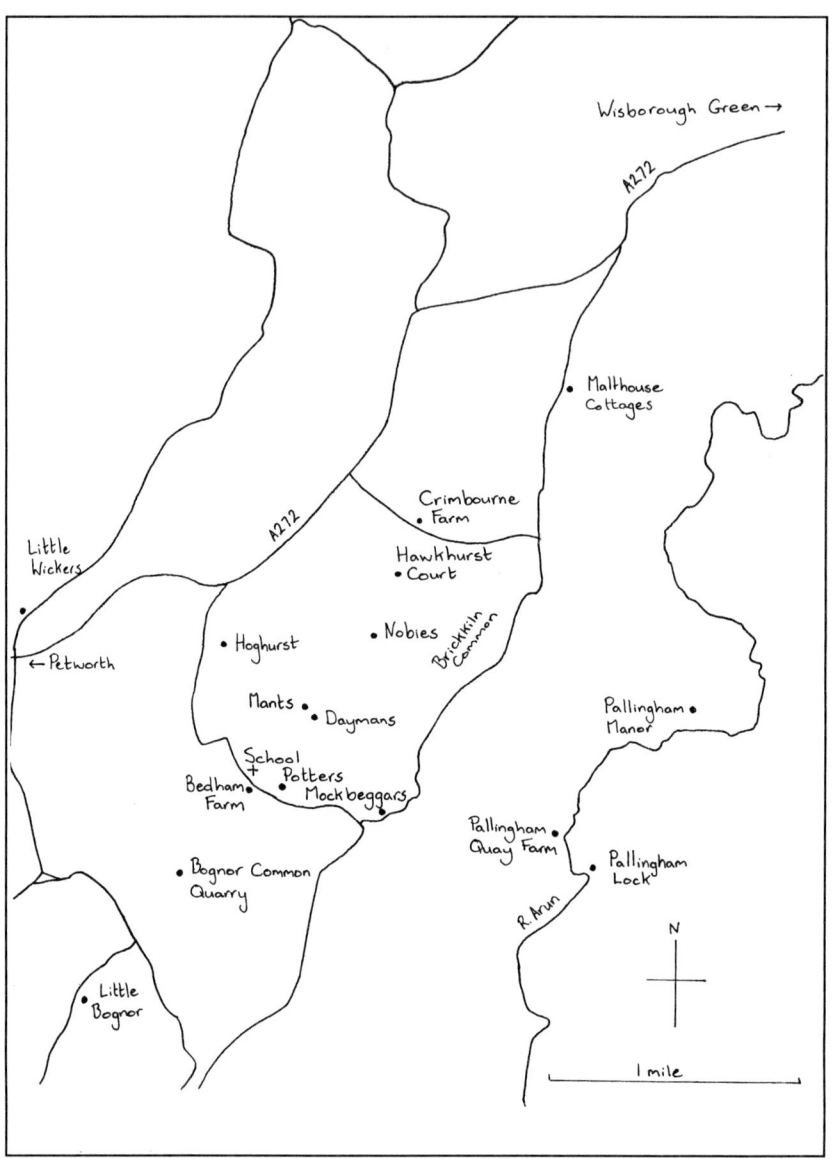

Map 2: Bedham and immediate area, location of places mentioned in the text.

HONOUR THY FATHER

You can't put old heads on young shoulders. I wonder how many times I heard my parents say that when I was a child?

It's never too late to mend;
Charity should begin at home;
He who hesitates looses;

and one which always seems so contradictory on top of all that 'look before you leap'. Not to mention all the superstitions I lapped up and which kept me scared stiff for years. Now, thank God, I have quite an old head on my shoulders and can look around and wish I could make the youngsters of today realize how lucky they are with their wonderful chances at school.

Without boasting, I can honestly say that I was quite bright at school in everything but maths. But there we all were, my sisters and brother stuck in Bedham Woods where we had a lovely wild sort of life but no chances to pick and choose our careers as children have today. The sad point of it, it is all taken for granted, and only a few seem to me to make an effort to get on. I often wonder who moulds children's lives most, parents or their teachers. Mine was a wonderful old lady and it's taken the old head of mine on old shoulders to appreciate her at all. I sometimes wonder whether going back to Bedham for nearly 17 (to me short) years has made me feel that I failed my teacher.[1] Perhaps too, it makes me think what a little horror I was, and how I smashed a slate and dashed home when she hit my sister. How on my return she made me stand on a form everyday at playtime for a fortnight. The day the Rector[2] came in and saw me I was allowed to sit until he went away.

I wonder too, whether I have been stupid to do what I have done,

---

[1] Caroline Day Headmistress Bedham School from 1894 to 1920
[2] Rev George Stuart Newbury MA Rector of Fittleworth 1900-1920

1

spending so much time with my father? I don't know that I am any more of a 'Fuddy Duddy' than other people who, when one parent dies, make the other give up home and live elsewhere.

Over the years I have gleaned a lot of stories about my father and his people, and have made notes of it all. I have learned also that the old saying 'It's no good getting old if you don't get artful' is quite true, for a more artful baggage than my father never existed. He has got an answer for everything. He makes me think of Bernard Thompson's

George Elliott aged 65 in his "old Trilby Hat".

Uncle Jim in 'Love in Quiet Places'[3], for my father's slogan which he was taught by an old man at an early age 'No good tellin' a lie if you don't stick to it', has stood him in good stead, and though I love him very much I know he can tell me a lie without batting an eyelid. He always agrees that the 'good die young' and I'm sure he sincerely believes that.

Now he is coming up for ninety-three,[4] and spends most of his time huddled up in the chimney corner, mostly with an old rusty, once navy blue, raincoat fastened with string across

---

[3] a novel published by Hodder and Stoughton in 1961
[4] George Elliott was 93 in 1963, he was born on 31.10.1870

2

his chest, and flying like a large bat when he walks about his living room. He lives in an old Trilby hat from the time he plods down the stairs until bedtime.

For the last 18 months I have slept there most nights. I have only one night off and through the bad winter I had no time off at all. He says he can't stay there another winter because I got ill with flu as soon as the thaw set in and had to have a fortnight away; during which time a sister obliged. When he talks like that I feel very sad, for I love Bedham and as the cottage belongs to a gentleman in London, I've had my chips so far as Bedham is concerned. I hope the old saying 'when one door shuts another one opens' will apply in my case. I don't understand my sisters, for there's only one beside myself who waits on my father on Wednesdays and I think she enjoys it.

My father was born at a place called 'Little Wickers' near Petworth, he was born on the 31st of October. His mother was a very frail woman, who died the year I was born.[5] I always envy people who enjoy their grandmothers. I am one myself and derive great pleasure from it despite suffering from being told "you spoil them so Mum."

When my father was born his mother had a dreadful time it seems and refused to sleep with my grandfather again. So they led very unhappy lives in consequence, what a difference today with the family planning centres.

When my father was 9 months old, his people moved to a cottage at Crimbourne where he caught a chill on the damp floors, which affected his legs and at 4 he was unable to walk. They moved to Mants Cottage[6] where he still lives today. One day a gypsy called and she took a look at the little boy who couldn't walk and said to his mother "You'll never rear that child, he's got water on the brain."

---

[5]   George's Mother Emily Elliott nee Whitington died 1906 aged 72
[6]   the Elliott family moved to Mants, Bedham in winter 1874 or early 1875

3

His father made up his mind to take him to Brighton to see what could be done for his legs. He had to carry him on his shoulders 6 miles to Pulborough station. The little boy who is my father was fitted with irons and with two sticks he managed to get around until he was 7 years old. And after that he was all right but never grew much.[7] He should of have done because both his parents were tall he says. I don't agree with that because I have three short sisters and I heard him talk about one of his relatives who was short but could put a sack of wheat on a horse's back without any trouble.

He had a very varied education, going from one old lady's cottage to another until Bedham School was built. He was 10 years of age he tells me and well remembers the wonderful party given by the gentleman who had it built.[8]

As a boy my father was rather lonely because of getting around with his irons and it seems they were mostly oldish people who lived at Bedham. The neighbours were very kind to him and were always giving him food as he had an enormous appetite. If he'd just had a meal and then went over to Potters Cottage Mrs. Juggy Remnant[9] that lived there and was a good cook, would ask George if he'd eaten and he would say no and have another good feed. I fancy he spent a good deal of time there and as he got older helped them in the garden. They always had plenty of wine on the go too, which was just up his alley.

My father had, and still has, a wonderful sense of humour and when he was at Potter's one day, a daughter was home on holiday from her domestic job. She was sitting in the old chimney corner when a wasp stung her in the groin. It was unusual in those days to see a bit of leg, and this girl tossed her clothes up over her head and squealed, but

---

[7]   George Elliott was just over 5' tall
[8]   Bedham School was built by Wm Townley Mitford of Pitshill and opened in 1880
[9]   Mrs Sarah Remnant wife of William Remnant

remembered George Elliott was there and was horrified. Her brother winked at George and George chuckled to himself you bet.

How I envy those people who can sit and write, sew or paint or whatever they wish to do without seeing all the housework wants attention, or cooking must be done. They have their minds above all that sort of thing, but poor me, having worked for years before and after marriage slaving away at housework, must have a ghost of one of my late mistress's watching over me and threatening one with dismissal if I sit around when there is so much to be done. Those early years of one's life, from school leaving till 21 at any rate, make an awful impression I'm sure for I stayed in one job for 6 years and just can't write until I've done the necessary cleaning and cooking. My father thinks I'm quite mad when I fetch the mats up daily but doesn't understand that I and my sisters were all made to do it and can't get out of the habit.

When I listen to my father sometimes, I'm driven to arguing about some of the things he tells me and I'm not surprised that a gentleman who lived at Bedham since my mother died called me notorious, for I'm only my father's daughter. If ever I live as long as he has (which I very much doubt) I wonder whether I'll be like the riddle of his

'How many sides are there to a Roly Poly Pudding?'

The answer is inside and outside.

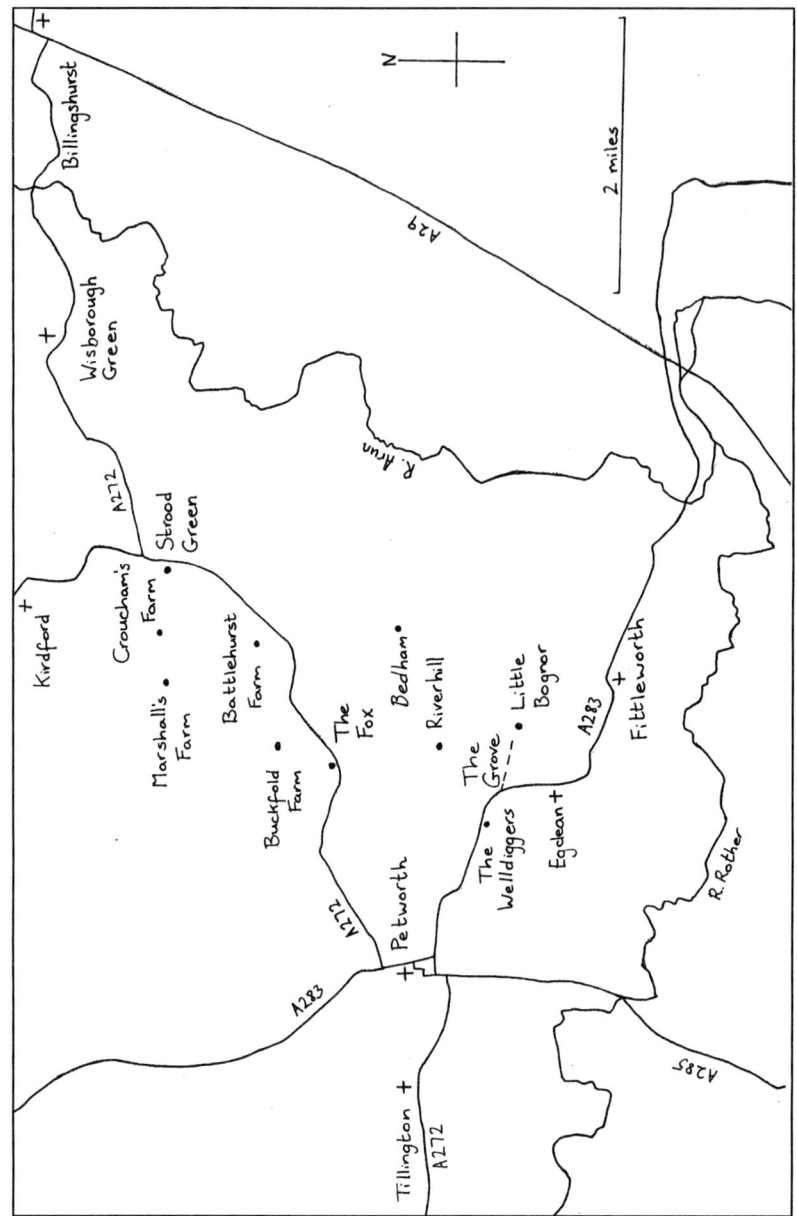

Map 3: Bedham and the wider area, location of places mentioned in the text.

He sits up in that chimney corner looking very docile and that's all his visitors know of him. But I've got to know the inside of his mind and I can never be a 'Yes woman' like my sister.

I think living at Bedham, surrounded by oldish people, encouraged him or, shall I say, moulded him, and made him wise long before he grew up. One lady who lived opposite and had no children used to have him over there for company, and feed him on all kinds of foods, She was a very hard working woman and went to great trouble in cooking. She used to buy pigs Chittlings.[10] and thoroughly clean them and fill them with Xmas Pudding mixture, boil them for a long time, when cold tie them up and hang them up the chimney, cutting a few at a time when required. My father said they were delicious.

One lady who lived in that cottage, used to work very hard and dig the garden from end to end and when her husband came home at night he'd say: "What you bin doin' with yerself all day, looking in the mirror to see yerself starve."
He was very hard.

My father had a sister 6 years his senior but she didn't get on so well with the neighbours regarding food, and I don't think she got on with my father, for as children we didn't know that we'd got an aunt at all.[11] I suspect her nose was just put out of joint when he was born.

When my father was small his grandfather on his mother's side lived with them at Bedham. I'm always interested in what my Dad's grandfather had for breakfast. He always used a wooden bowl, into which he cut up bread and about 2oz of Butter and a nice helping of sugar then filled the bowl and its contents up with boiling hot tea. He

---

[10] the smaller intestine of beasts… sometimes filled with mincement or forcemeat : OED
[11] Eliza Elliott born 1865. She lived with her parents at Malt Houses, Wisborough Green and died at Petworth in 1934

7

used to beat it up well before eating it. He was a great sufferer of indigestion I've been told and I'm not surprised. This old man was what in the old days was called a "come by chance" which means illegitimate and his father had to pay his mother 1/6d. per week until he was 7 years of age. At the end of that time his father was allowed to claim him and when the day came the boy was in a copse with his grandfather who was copse cutting. The old man refused to part with the boy. So they decided to fight for him and stripped down, did just that. The old man won the day and so the boy stayed with his grandfather. If his father had won the fight the boy would have been sent to sea.[12]

Going back to my father's grandfather living at Bedham with his daughter and son-in-law: times were a bit different than they are now for all the old man was allowed was 1/- and a bag of flour which had to be fetched from Fittleworth.[13] My father always says how wonderful it is to have a weekly pension and so enable old people to be independent of their off-spring. Many a sad story he has told me about where old men and women have fared very sadly. One old man who was a bit simple lived in a copse and when he was too old to earn a few shillings went to the river and caught a fish and toasted it over his camp fire. Of course in my father's time there was the workhouse but many of the old people just couldn't bear it. One man he knew that had lost his wife advertised for a housekeeper after getting in an awful state with fleas etc. He took the first one who applied and why my father remembers her so well, she sat a goose on eggs that were infertile and nobody could make her believe that a gander was necessary. She wore her hair in corkscrew curls down over her shoulders. They came to a sad end through lack of money.

My great grandfather[14] who lived at Bedham as I've already stated told

---

[12] See Appendix 1 – Come-by-chance and the fight in the copse
[13] possibly distributed through Lee's Charity of Fittleworth
[14] Lillian's Great Grandfather John Whitington was born in 1798

8

my father stories which had been handed down from one generation to another by Whitingtons. Going back to the days of my great great great grandfather when men were pressed to go to war[15] and the story is fresh in my father's mind today, how this man was in Petworth on Saturday night and he had his wife with him. He was taken by two soldiers on entering the Wheatsheaf Pub in North Street. They took him in between them into the chimney corner and different people kept treating the soldiers to drinks until they fell asleep and the prisoner escaped with his wife only to be taken again before they got to the end of North Street. In those days men always took a boy with them and on entering Petworth with a cart load of stuff to be delivered would crawl under a cover and let the boy take charge of the load. Even then they were caught and taken off sometimes.

One of my father's ancestors worked at Marshalls Farm for Downers who farmed it for hundreds of years.[16] He was a big handsome man named Will[17] and he very much hated going to the French War. So Mr. Downer used to tease him by calling on Sunday mornings at his cottage and saying he'd got his papers. At last one day he had got his papers and Will had to go. He told the recruiting people that he'd got a bad back and they put something on it which blistered it and then he really

---

[15] Lillian's Great Great Great Grandfather was born c.1743 and died in 1828. The seizing of men to impress (i.e force) them into naval service was practised during the Napoleonic Wars, it is therefore quite possible that he did hear of, or even know of cases of impressment. Gardiner & Wenborn state the practice "was largely abandoned after the French Revolutionary and Napoleonic Wars (1793-1815)".

[16] The 1841 Census shows John Downer at Marshalls, Kirdford. Documents in the Cowdray Archive show a Thomas Downer farming in Kirdford in 1753, further documents in the WSRO show a John Downer holding land at Billingshurst in 1721.

[17] the Whitington family had long established links with Marshalls Farm, this was possibly Letitia Whitington's brother William born c.1783

9

did have a bad back. After serving 5 years his commanding officer came to him and put 50 Gold Sovereigns on the drum and said, "These are yours if you'll serve another 5 years" but Will said "No." So badly as he wanted money he longed to go home.

When my Great Grandfather Whitington was young he worked on a farm at a little place under the Downs somewhere around Storrington[18] and the farmer used to send him to Worthing for seaweed, which I gather was spread on the land. One night when a girl my grandmother asked if she might go with him. He said yes and decided to make an early start. The old lady next door was a queer bird I'm told so they never mentioned to anyone about going and got up at 3 am. Crept out as quietly as they could and harnessed the horses and were just going out of the gates when the old lady poked her head out of her window and said, "My how the sea do roar."

While still living on that farm my great grandfather was asked to take an entire horse[19] to the fair at Egdean, near Petworth. It wasn't his job but the man who had been looking after the horse committed suicide, previously having said he would do just that if the horse became his master. Great grandfather was very daring and also very courageous and went off to the fair only to be told on arrival that he was to take the horse away at once before it killed somebody, so off he went again taking his time and getting a drink at various Pubs on the way home. His wife got very anxious by evening and sent some of her children up a field overlooking the lane approaching the farm to see if he was coming. They ran back to their mother and said they'd seen him coming along sitting on the horse's back humming a tune. The farmer sold the horse and the next man that looked after it was kicked and torn to pieces by it and so it had to be destroyed.

---

[18] The 1841 Census shows John Whitington and his family at Sullington Lane Cottage, Sullington near Storrington
[19] a stallion : JG

Great Grandfather told my father that there really was a small town on Egdean Common and that a Golden Calf was lost somewhere between Egdean and the downs. I wish it could be excavated to prove his words. It used to be a wonderful fair and the corner beyond the Well Diggers has always been known as "Plum Pudding Corner" because Plum Puddings were sold on fair day at that corner.[20]

Great Grandfather's next move was to Watersfield and that was how my Grandfather Elliott came into contact with them. He was born at Cootham and got lodging with the Whitingtons at Watersfield (I think they kept a Pub) when the railway was laid from Pulborough to Petworth etc.[21] When he married[22] he always lived with the in laws. I can't help feeling sorry for my grandfather and think that he had a raw deal one way and another. I love listening to my father about his childhood days for it was a queer set up and no mistake. When his mother and family moved from Watersfield they took a Beer House[23] as my father calls it in Lombard Street which later became a Bakers shop now Antiques. From there they moved to 'Little Wickers.'

Before they took over Mants Cottage there was a sale in the garden. Quite a big do he says and had a Beer booth and food served in tents etc and a crowd of people gathered there and made a day of it. Of course a furniture sale etc always means a sad day for someone and the reason for this sale was that the Tenant, an old man, had died[24] and there was only a son left and I understand from my father that the landlord did not allow bachelors to live alone in a cottage so he'd notice to quit. He was so bitter at leaving the lovely garden

---

[20] Egdean fairs were held annually on 1st May & 4th September and "are much frequented for the sale of cattle and sheep" : Dallaway
[21] the Pulborough/Petworth line opened on 15th October 1859
[22] George Elliott Snr & Emily Whitington married at Coldwaltham on 30th May, 1863
[23] a house licenced to sale beer, but not spirits : OED
[24] James Sebbage who died November 1874 aged 74

and orchard which was full of fruit trees that he had his revenge on the future tenants by removing the turf around some of the trees and sawing them almost through and then replacing the turf. On the day of the sale it was discovered and the culprit was obliged to clear right out of the district as in those days it was a very serious offence. I've heard my father say the warrant for his arrest was renewed at intervals for 21 years.

After my grandparents moved in someone was known to have asked a woman who lived opposite how she liked her new neighbours and she scornfully replied, "Neighbours near livers you mean." That was because hitherto people had made a regular path through grandmother's garden and my grandmother fenced it up.

My father has often told me she would never borrow and always said the first shift was the best one. She was always very poor because of the unhappy way of living separate lives caused my grandfather to turn to beer for consolation. He never bothered about other women.

When my grandmother ran out of tea and had no money to get any she would toast a piece of bread until it was almost black and pour boiling water on it and drink it as tea.[25] My father has never eaten a bit of toast in my memory. His mother was very thrifty in every way making her own vinegar with black currants. I think my father was very devoted to her and always did his best to protect her in his father's absence. So well did he look after her that he used to take the "Muzzle loader'[26] to bed with him and when he was about eleven years old they went to bed a bit fidgety as they thought they heard someone about. During the night his mother roused him saying, "George there's someone in the garden at our chicken or trying to get in for something."
George was up like a shot and balancing the gun on the window ledge

---

[25] known as Donkey Tea : DSD
[26] a gun "which is designed to be loaded at the muzzle end… invariably either designs of or guns that date from the 18th century - Hansard

he called out "Who's there?' No answer. He said "If you don't speak up I shall shoot after the third time." Presently his father said "Not much the matter Reckon." Which was a favourite saying of his. That was a narrow squeak I guess.

His father was very clever with animals and quite a vet in his way although he had no training. I think largely it was a gift that he had and added to that he gleaned a lot of knowledge from a man who it seems was a Vet but used to drink such a lot that most times he hadn't a shirt to his back and would go about with what my father calls a bobtail[27] coat, buttoned right up in the hottest of weather. My opinion, he was a good man even if he did drink such a lot. According to my father people wouldn't send for him because they were ashamed to see him on their farms etc. All sorts of people used to send for my grandfather. Whenever he was in residence at Mants Cottage somebody would call for him and off he'd go without any breakfast and wait on some sick animal and all he would get was a drink or two and no profitable work done that day.

My grandfather kept a cow and one thing about the cow interests me very much. When my father was a boy he was told that all oxen in stables got up and turned round at midnight on old Xmas night, 6th January.[28] One night his parents and grandfather made up their minds to prove it, so they all sat up on the old chimney corner (drinking wine I expect) and looked up across the garden where the cow (she was white) could been seen getting up and she did a turn round and laid down again.

---

[27] "having the tail cut short" : Webster. Therefore a coat with no tails, a short coat or jacket JG
[28] the Gregorian Calendar was introduced in 1752 making a change of 11 days. Lillian's family were therefore still remembering the old pre 1752 Xmas night at least 125 years after the calendar change. It is interesting how strongly and accurately the change is recalled even after such a long period.

I think my grandfather was a hardworking man and taught my father at a very early age to use a scythe and fag-hook[29] and tree rinding[30] etc. Some of the older men weren't very keen on training young boys tree felling, rinding and so on and my grandfather would have them wished on him. When this happened one day he took a look at the boy in question and said, "If you want to get on and learn you'll have to take the quart loaves from under your arms I can tell ye."[31]

While writing about my father's boyhood days I must say a few words about a very interesting gentleman who farmed Battlehurst[32] and other surrounding farms. He was very eccentric but very just I feel. When he employed boys he would never allow them to work close together but spread them out in far corners of the fields saying:
"One boy is a boy, two boys half a boy, 3 boys no boy at all."
I have learned from experience it is quite true. One day a man called on this farmer saying he'd heard he wanted an extra hand. The farmer looked him over and said,
"Hmm Ah, Well Tick Tick Tee
  call again Thursday
  and I'll let you know."
In the mean time he made enquiries about the man and on Thursday night when he called again he (the farmer) opened the door to him and said,
"Hmm Ah Well, Tick, Tick Tee
  you might suit some people
  but you won't suit me.
  Good night."
and shut the door.

My mother used to do the laundry for the Farmer's Widow and I and

---

[29] a hook fastened on a long stick for trimming hedges : DSD
[30] stripping the bark from felled oak trees for use in tanning leather : DSD
[31] stop standing around with your hands on your hips and start working : JG
[32] John Eede who farmed Battlehurst from at least 1841

one of my sisters used to fetch and take it and it nearly killed us the weight of it. The lady used to hate ginger cats and ours used to follow us over there and if she saw it she'd shreek, "Take it away I don't like Yellow cats."

As children my sisters and I used to go over to Battlehurst Farm in the moonlight and slide on the pond in winter. The carter who was working there at the time taught us how to do it by hanging onto his coat tail and we soon learned to balance ourselves. The old farmer had died by then or he would never have allowed it. He always rode around on horse back to his various farms and would tell his horse everything he was going to say to his men when he arrived. The horse's ears would go up and down and the animal would become so interested in the conversation that it would almost stop and then the Farmer would say, "Go on horse."

Only last week my father was asked if he believed in witches etc and he said he didn't know. But he is inclined to believe such things did happen to make one wonder. When he was a boy he went with his sister to work on a farm at Little Bognor. My father has always loved horses etc and he was given the job to lead the horses with the loaded wagon and then go back and change over while another boy looked after the horse that had to keep moving while being loaded with hay. Women and children all helped with the haying and at night they would all have a ride on the wagons through the Grove and one night while going through there the horses stopped dead and refused to budge. The carter didn't say anything but got down off his wagon and opened his pocket knife and ran the blade round all the spokes in turn and after that the horses started off again. My father tells me the story how if you go through the Grove at a certain time of night one is supposed to see Oranges[33] dancing in the Grove.

There used to be a cottage on a hillside about halfway through the

---

[33] this is probably a reference to Jack O'Lanterns

15

Grove. The woman who lived there used to make corduroy trousers. My grandfather used to buy them as they were very satisfactory and very cheap too. The cottage caught fire and was quite destroyed. I always feel sad about old cottages which are allowed to fall down or are pulled down for they have much more character than the modern ones ever will have. My father wouldn't leave his old tumble down cottage for a mansion.

My father and his sister used to go gleaning[34] at Little Bognor also. After the Wheat had been cut they were allowed to do this. When they had a sackful of wheat my grandfather used to go and fetch it to Mants Barn at Bedham and thrash, tout[35] then carry it back to Little Bognor Mill to be ground into flour. How spoilt every body, even the working class are today.

When my father was a boy he used to spend a lot of his time at Nobies where there was a large family.[36] He spent a lot of time with them and he has told me how wonderfully well brought up they were and well spoken and it always amazed him when he saw the boys remove their caps when people visited the house and so on. He and the boys used to go Wassailling at Xmas time practising for weeks before hand. They used to go round all the farmhouses and choose their songs to suit the people. They always got plenty of wine and food. My father had a wonderful voice.

One night on his return from Nobies he had quite a shock. It was a lovely clear starlight night and presently all the stars seemed to tumbledown around him. He says he was about sixteen at the time. The next day a gentleman called on his mother and told her he was very sad to have missed the shower of Meteors. My father had told my grandparents about it. They didn't see it and my father when told was

---

[34] to pick up ears of corn left by the reapers : OED
[35] to toss or throw about in disorder : OED - as in winnowing JG
[36] Emund Johnson a hoopmaker, his wife Ellen and their 8 children

only too pleased to have an explanation of the queer thing which had happened.

Having glanced over what I hope to be quite an interesting story of my father's life until now I've decided to copy what I have written down since he was ninety years of age. My life over the last sixteen or seventeen years has been so mixed up with his that it is the only way. When I was young I heard so many a time "Honour thy father" and I can honestly say I have done just that and if this ever gets printed it shall be the title of my book.

I think my father is always proud to say that he only had one love which of course was my mother and I know, although she spoilt him in every way, he loved her very much and they had a very happy life together. They met when he was working at Tillington and when they were married they lived in North Street[37] in which he made me understand there were some cottages known as "Rabbit Hutch Row", when I asked him about it recently he said it was only a name he gave them.

While living there he had a variety of jobs, one being delivering paraffin with a donkey cart. He went miles with it selling it at 9d. a gallon. The old man whose business it was had too much to drink one day and fell out of the cart. My father enjoyed the job very much, it was child's play to what he was normally used to. Another job was labouring for the man who put up the Gasometer,[38] He had ¼ an hour more than the other chaps to hold the rivets which were put in the seams to hold up the Gasometer and one had a very narrow ledge to

---

[37] Petworth

[38] the Gasometer was in Station Road. A letter from George Elliott to his daughter Olive in 1956 relates how the original Gasometer was replaced in 1892 by 'a firm from Sheffield'. It was at this time that he worked on the gasometer as 'the foreman's mate..' The Gasometer was demolished in 1963

Letter from George Elliott dated 20.11.56 to his Daughter Olive regarding the Petworth gasometer.

work on. A man would often dodge off[39] after his meal and with arms folded nod off and always save himself from falling into the water when his feet hit up against the metal ledge.

After that they moved to Crouchams at Kirdford and Kirdford was one of the worst places for work in those days, now it is flourishing with fruit orchards and Pack Houses. The year my father went to Crouchams it was a very dry hot summer and nothing doing anywhere not a drop of rain from March to August.[40] My father said he met a man one day who had just left a job at Little Bognor. Waring and Gillows[41] were doing a big job there in the building line. So off rushed my father and his luck was in and he started straight away. There was a gang of Londoners and they had their food cooked on the spot and a beer barrel on the go all the time. They set my father to be cook and of course it worried him at first but he soon got used to it. After being nearly starved for weeks he ate so much food that he was quite ill for days. Only sheer determination pulled him through it. Many a tit-bit he took home to my mother. He used to sing all the way home to Crouchams. People used to tell my mother they could hear him coming. He must have been very happy, I'm sure he was.

He has often told me how he came to get the cottage at Bedham. His father got behind with the rent and he heard about it and told his parents and they got windy[42] and packed up and went to live at Malt House Cottages.[43] After about 4 years the cottage became vacant and my father went to see the Landlord and got it. Until this day he regrets

---

[39] to avoid work by use of any semi-legimate excuse : OED
[40] 1893. "The drought which prevailed over England and the neighbouring parts of the Continent during the spring and summer of 1893 was so exceptional, both as regards severity and duration..." : Brodie
[41] a company designing and manufacturing very high class furniture. Founded in 1903.
[42] scared - JG
[43] at Wisborough Green

ever having a word to his mother for she hated leaving the cottage and when all the furniture had been removed she sat all alone in the cottage for nearly a week on a three legged stool. Poor darling I feel for her very much.

Two of my seven sisters were born at Crouchams and the rest at Bedham, nine of us, eight daughters and one son at the end of the line. How my mother doted on him I can never forget.

My eldest sister had a dreadful time when she was a schoolgirl and my father always said she was bewitched at the time for she had dreadful nightmares and grew quite ill always saying she could see him in the trees. When a certain old man died she slept for several days and it frightened my parents but her health improved after that and it was more or less forgotten.

One reads and hears such a lot about hygiene and modern homes these days to house families but when I think of all us children living in that tumble down cottage and the old well of water it makes me laugh. There was a large family born opposite us too. The parents came there in my father's youth and did he love all those boys and girls and when he got married and finally came back to his old home he had a lovely time with the boys over the way. I know one of the sons and he visits my father frequently and says he's never so happy as when he sits in the old chimney corner talking over old times.

My father during his life time has worked at all sorts of jobs to make a living. Everybody living in cottages like those at Bedham had a sty and kept pigs and took them to market in pony traps etc. Often my mother would hob up[44] some by the living room fire that a farmer's wife or someone gave her and my father says how wonderful mother was to get up in the night to feed them and stoke the fire to keep them warm. She

---

[44] to bring up anything (an animal) by hand : DSD

20

always got up first and in tree felling and Rinding time[45]she'd be out of bed at 4 am, get a meal ready for him to be out in the woods at 5 am, then take out another meal and a can of tea some times having to walk quite a distance. He always says what a wonderful wife he had but I wonder whether he ever told her so. I very much doubt it.[46]

Having children in those days wasn't funny, no district nurses or Nursing homes but some old or middle aged woman who did the best she could. One had too much to drink and fell down the stairs. One baby my father just had to deliver himself. But by all accounts he was very good and fetched the doctor. It was wonderful how some women survived childbirth. My father told me a story of some very poor people who lived at Hoghurst. The woman was in labour and the man came over to see whether my mother could help but she was in bed with a new baby so father got up and in horrible misty rain he and the anxious man tried cottage after cottage in vain until at last an old lady very reluctantly got up and off they went and on arriving found there was simply nothing to use, no baby clothes, no anything. The poor woman was lying on the floor, no bed, no furniture. So my father and the old lady had to find their way back to her cottage and collect some things and go back again. He said they were wandering about all night.

By the time I arrived my eldest sisters were out to work and the eldest on hearing she had another sister said. "I'm not going home." But she did, bless her.

I love to hear my father say that if he had his time over again he'd do just the same. Marry young and have a normal married life. He says the prevention of children is what fills the divorce courts. Husband and wife should let things take their natural course. When I think of my poor mother and what a hard life she had I can't help disagreeing with

---

[45] in spring when the sap is rising
[46] Martha Elliott nee Stevens died 4th September 1946 - 27 years before her husband

21

him. It's the woman who suffers every time I say. He says my mother never complained and I don't believe she did for when she was dying (she was only ill one weekend) all she kept worrying about was, "I'm keeping you all away from your husbands."

I'm proud of her and my wonderful memory of her. Making all our clothes, refooting socks, cooking all our meals, making all our bread in the old brick oven. I've seen her in summer with the perspiration pouring down her face, raking the hot embers out of the oven before putting the bread, cakes, pies, milk puddings etc in it. We were always hovering round when it was due to be taken out you may depend, and my mother used to make little cottage loaves which could be taken out early and we'd eat them hot with a nice dab of butter in between. She used to make lovely rabbit pies and somehow the food had a different flavour.

We had to work very hard as children fetching the wood to put in the old brick oven and other jobs besides. I used to hate Mondays and Tuesday when I got in from school and saw my mother and the washing she'd got through. She did two large laundry baskets full every week. When I think it all over I just don't know how my mother did it.

We had two large cherry trees in our garden at Mants and my grandfather planted them. They used to have a wonderful crop of cherries on them and we all had to take turns getting up at 4 am to wander about and keep the birds away. I well remember feeling quite ill trying to keep my eyes open, never mind the birds. It was awful. Our reward was 3/6d. to spend at Wisborough Green. My father used to pick them and take them in a donkey cart to Wisborough Green and pitch up outside the Three Crowns, at that time it was open all day I expect.

Dr. Barnardo's Home used to send a lot of children to Wisborough

Green each year and they camped on the green, I think I am right in saying. They were very good customers.

While on the subject of father and his donkey cart, one of the boys opposite (they were grown up by the time I was born) was playing at the top of Bedham when my father one day was on his way to Fittleworth with his donkey and cart. When he saw the boy he asked him if he would like a ride. He said yes and jolly soon hopped up into the cart. It was a very hot day and when they'd got part of the way to Fittleworth the boy suddenly said "I can't go Mas' Elliott, I've got Granny's hat on." He went after taking the hat off. Years later he came back to have a look round his old home and spotting my father working in a gentleman's garden shouted out; "I ain't got Granny's hat on today, Mas' Elliott."

I think those boys opposite enjoyed my father more than their own father. One Sunday morning my father and theirs went off for a walk over the Bognor Common while their wives were cooking the beef steak puddings. It was a regular Sunday dinner at Bedham, pudding, veg, potatoes all cooked in one large pot over the open fire place. While the men were dawdling along one of the boys came along and said, "Mas Elliott don't know what I knows."
His father said, "Damm sure he don't. What ye mean Reg?" and he repeated again, "Mas Elliott don't know what I knows, his chimneys on fire."
This young man will never be forgotten by my father, or his brother for he had such a sunny disposition and was always teasing people. He was killed in World War I.[47]

Bedham was alive with people in those days and when I went to school there were over sixty children attending.

---

[47] the Boxall family of Daymans Cottage. Reg Boxall was killed while serving with Royal Sussex Regiment

Photo of Bedham school pupils, circa 1914.
Top row, extreme right – Lavender and Alice Elliott
Second row, third from right – Charlie Hunt, Lillian Elliott's future husband
Bottom row, extreme left – Lillian, George and Myrtle Elliott

As I have stated previously my father learned from his father all kinds of work. He couldn't bear him to learn cartering as he called it for he said "following a horse's tail all day was awful", so he used to do cow minding at first and this he enjoyed and used to go off with his whistle pipe all around the commons. One day he was sitting on a gate just about to eat his mid-day snack when a tramp came along. He was a bit scared but when he got too close (he could see the man after his food) he picked up his stick, which he always had with him, and swiped it across the man's shoulders and he slunk off. My father cleared out too he said and met a man who had been breaking stones by the roadside and told him about it. He said, "I'll lay he'll take my smock that I tucked in a bush way back." And so he had on looking for it.

One day my father got up a tree and changed his voice and annoyed an old man he looked after cows for and so got the sack. Another time he was talking to men in the stone quarry at Bognor Common when they spied their boss coming in the distance. They had paused in their work to listen to George but started making a noise as though ever so busy. When the boss got to them he said, "Who was that you was talking to just now?"
"Oh" said one, "that was George Elliott mindin' the cows."
"Oh was it" said the boss, "Well we don't want any telegraph news here let the boy get on with his cow mindin."

My father had a good training at digging, breaking and piling stone. Although they do stone and rubble today they don't have to pile them. In the old days they had to be paid by the yard and I think I'm right in saying square yards for they were piled beautifully. It was quite an art I'm sure and to me rather stupid because once piled and the men paid they were taken away so to me it seems a loss of time, piling.

When my father was fourteen he was temporally out of a job and went to the quarries where two men were digging but hadn't a clue how to pile so George was taken on to do it for them. He earned 6/- a week and

Bedham School circa 1910 with the headmistress Miss Day centre and Miss Laura Wakeford on right.

26

enjoyed doing it and was sorry when the job ran out. In those days for the most part each season had its job either haying, harvesting, copse cutting, river cleaning or something. That's why my father knew so many jobs. The stories he has told me of different men he worked with and how they used to cheat and not do the job properly. Even he was a dab hand at taking the easy way out for one year when he went with his father grass cutting he hit on the bright idea that instead of all having a cant[48] each as he calls it that is, cut so wide and keeping going to the other end of the meadow, he suggested they cut in a circle and he'd be the last one so that he cut less every time. He thought it was a great joke.

After he was married he used to go in a gang including his father and a farmer said "My, how that boy of yours can swing a scythe." He'd got several children by that time.

He wasn't always happy about cheating, for a fellow took a job with him thatching a hay rick. The farmer helped to measure the rick to tell how much money they had to draw. To do this a measure (or rope I gather) was tossed over, the farmer holding one end and the mate of my father the other. He pulled it down much further than he ought but the farmer twigged it. I think farmers used to pay out a lot even in those days for most of them found beer or cider and food.

I'm most interested in the way farmers at Arundel used to get their men or quite a few of them when grass was ready to be cut. Tramps and what have you, women included, used to line up on the Bridge by the station and farmers would come and pick how many they wanted.[49] In the morning after the start my father said you could see the hay cocks[50] move and people would come crawling out and go into Arundel to

---

[48] a corner of a field or a division of land or work : DSD
[49] this practise continued into the early 20th century : Mr F Penfold pers.comm
[50] a conical heap of hay in the field : OED

get breakfast or early tea. I spose[51] they could buy it, people were expecting them. My father and his gang used to get a lodge if possible, failing that a granary at a farm. They had no trouble to get work while the haying and harvesting lasted. From what I can gather he used to enjoy it but was always pleased when Saturday night came to get home to his wife. The walking they did in those days puts us all to shame now. We all have petrol feet.[52]

I feel I was born 40 years too soon for my education and father feels he was born too soon because he would love to have driven something. For years he kept telling me you couldn't beat an old horse and cart but now I am sure he thinks differently. The stories he's told me how people treated horses makes me shudder. When he was a boy some people lived up above them and the man starved his horses and every now and then one died or he had to have it destroyed. He used to keep them in a stable and they even ate their racks which should have had food in and when his wife had a baby she got up after three days and went out with a scythe and cut grass for them. My grandfather used to skin the dead horses after digging a hole to bury the horse he'd drag the skin on his back all the way to the Tanners at Petworth[53] where he would receive the large sum of 7/6d. The man that kept the horses used to boast to people, patting his son's head and saying "We looked out for a rainy day didn't we boy." But it didn't last for it leaked out that a brother had supplied him with horses and that came to a sudden end.

My father tells me that when they worked at Arundel there was a butcher who sold cooked meat. It was very useful to them and he often says he can't think why they don't do it now for it would be a great help to old people. He also tells me that when he was young people could take their joint of meat to a baker's shop on Sundays to be

---

[51] suppose
[52] George Elliott's expression for relying too much on cars rather than walking
[53] in East Street, Petworth

28

roasted and the bakers would charge 1d. per lb of meat. I think it was a wonderful idea especially in the festive seasons when perhaps one's joint needed a larger oven. While on the story of meat I must relate what happened to a publican's wife who kept the Red Lion.[54] She used to cook her beef steak pudding in a large pot over the open fire in the bar parlour, every now and then coming in to attend to the fire and make sure it kept boiling. While she was out of the room and the pudding was about cooked a couple of men took it out of the pot and made off with it having told a man who sat in there watching (and was a bit simple) what to say when the lady came in for it. She came in and found it gone and she asked the man who sat there who had the pudding and he said, "I know who had it but never had sense enough to keep it." She was livid with rage and accused him of having it and to use my father's words, he nearly got shopped up[55] over it. I can well imagine how frustrating it was to the lady who cooked it. Of course the men were never seen again.

Another amusing story he told me one day was about a man who was having a "drunken day" in what my father said used to be called the Swan Tap which was a part of the Swan Hotel.[56] I think it must have been at the back somewhere. This man was saying he hadn't any Baccy on him but he had plenty at home upon the clock. A man who had been listening took the trouble to walk out to Langhurst Hill and knocked on the door of the house where the tobacco was. The lady came to the door and the man said, "Your husband went away without his baccy this mornin' and he says its up on the clock."
The lady went in and fetched it, gave it to him and he went away laughing to himself. When her husband arrived home that evening the first thing he did on entering the house was to go to the clock and when he couldn't find it he said, "What have ye done with my Baccy

---

[54] corner of Middle and New Streets Petworth, now antiques
[55] to inform against a person so that he is arrested : Brewers
[56] the original Swan which formed the corner of Market Square and Saddlers Row in Petworth. It was demolished in 1899.

29

Missus?" She said "You sent a man for it this mornin' didn't ye and I let him have it." Poor man he was in a way you bet. Another man in a Pub, when he should have been at work was asked whether work and him had fallen out but he said, "No. We ain't fallen out 'cause we was never any friends."

Another Pub story was about a young man who had been brought up in the wilds and was told (on leaving home to go away to work) by his father to take care of himself and if he got cornered up in any fights or anything to show 'em he wasn't brought up in the woods to be frightened by an owl. So there came a time when he did find himself in a spot. He was in a Pub which was quite full of men of all sorts when he discovered someone had stolen his watch. He remembered his father's words and went straight to the door through which the men had to go, shut it, stood up against it and said in a loud voice so that everyone could hear, "Someone in this room has stolen my watch and I'm determined to find it and anybody who tries to get out of this door will be knocked down until I've got my watch." When they tried to get out he struck out at them left and right until one of them handed over his watch.

At this time of year my father always goes back to his young days and Tree Felling and Rinding. When he hears of the wages today and how they earn a lot he is very peeved for in the old days they cut the trees for nothing, all they got was for the bark[57] and cord wood[58]. It does seem a bit steep. He became what they call a ganger very young having been born with an axe in his hand as he loves to tell me. What he didn't like was how they used to shoe them as he called it. The gang would fix their man and get him down and hit the soles of his boots till he cried 'beer'. If you wouldn't say it you were fined 1/-.

---

[57] used in tanning leather

[58] the trimmings from the felled trees used for firewood "large pieces of wood, roots etc., set up in stacks. Cut to the cord length of 4ft or 3ft" : DSD

One of the men he worked with had a queer sense of humour but I also suspect he disliked my father. Any way one day when he found a bird's nest full of eggs he picked one up and threw it in my father's face and the yoke of it spilled down my father's cheeks. He has an awful temper like me when he is really roused, anyhow the man said he would stand a gallon of beer to make it right and it blew over. This man also had a frightful temper and his wife did too, you bet they were always quarrelling when together. One night he told her he'd go and jump into a pond which was a little way away from their cottage. So he rushed out, found a big stone, almost a boulder, and threw it out as far as he could. It made an almighty splash and rattle and his poor wife dashed out to see and found him there laughing fit to burst to think he'd given her such a fright. He told his mates one morning that the night before he'd gone out into a field and laid down and tried to die but he couldn't manage it. He was a very heavy drinker. This same man came to live opposite us when I was a school girl and the other large family had moved to Hoghurst, and I've never forgotten one night he offered a penny to the one who could make the ugliest face. Yours truly won the penny.

Seven of the Elliott sisters at Bedham 1914.

The son of this man told my mother he would take us girls (there were 4 of us left at home at that time) to a Carnival at Fittleworth which used to be held in one of the meadows opposite the Swan Hotel or a little way up the lane nearby. We were all decked up in white dresses trimmed with lace and blue sashes and off we went. We had a lovely time with James until the evening when, like his father, he kept drinking

31

which made us late starting for home. Eventually he got us up as far as Bognor Common and there he laid down. My father in the meantime went to bed but at 11 pm he got up and went out to look for us. Did he see Red[59] when he met us without James I wonder? Still we really did enjoy ourselves.

One night he (James) told his father and sister (his mother died before they came to Bedham) he would get back home between 2 and 3 am. Unknown to them he painted 2 on one gate and 3 on the other. Those figures stayed on there till the posts rotted away. James, I've been told killed himself with Beef Steak Pudding, having one made every day of his life after he married and got away. He died in the garden I heard.

I knew another man named Jim at Bedham and he was funny too in a different way. When my father was a boy his father took him to a wedding of one of Jim's relations and they were late getting there so never went to Church. When they went in the wee Bungalow my people found they'd all been drinking mead which is made from honeycomb out of the old fashioned bee skepps,[60] which were made of straw. The wedding guests one by one fell asleep and slithered down under the table. Grandfather took a look at them all and said, "We may as well get off home, boy."

My Grandmother Elliott used to make mead too and one day she gave in to her son George because he kept wanting some and when she wasn't looking he took another lot and all weekend he was quite dotty. So his father said on Monday morning "I'll take him up to Wisborough Green to get the doctor to have a look at him." They had just got him dressed up when he came to his senses. That finished my grandmother making mead.

My father has always been very bad about taking medicine and once he

---

[59] to be very angry : Brewers
[60] beehives : OED

32

tells me when he was a child and very poorly his mother said he must have some medicine. He refused to take it so his grandfather and father fixed him and one held him while the other pinched his nose so that his mother could pour the medicine down his throat but he bit a piece of glass right out of the tumbler and they gave up after that.

To go back to Jim of the mead. A gentleman was fixing up some sort of fence and was holding a pencil up at arm's length and squinting one eye and trying to make Jim understand what he wanted to do but without success. Presently the gentleman lost his wool[61] and said, "Well there is one thing we know and that is we have got one damm fool on the place."
And Jim says, "Ah to be sure, an' I could touch another one with a short stick."
The gentleman had a jolly good laugh for he was a good sort.

One day Jim went off round Bedham hill with the idea of going to tea with some friends. On his way a car pulled up and a man poked his head out of the window and said, "Can you tell me the way to Journeys-end please?"
Jim said, "Ah p'raps that'll be when you gets there, you'll know best 'bout that."
and the man said, "Seriously though can you tell us the way to Journeys-end?" and Jim repeated "Ah p'raps" again so they gave him 1/- for being funny and went on. The place they was looking for had changed its name and had they said Wakestone Cottage Jim could have helped them.

Jim had a brother who was queer[62] too, although my father said its what Jim made of him when their parents died and they were left to fend for themselves for Jim was horrid to his brother. Chaus had a donkey and cart and used to collect things from the station for people. Once he was

---

[61] lost his temper : S Goldsmith pers.comm
[62] strange - JG

seen on the way up from Fittleworth sitting up in the donkey cart with a trunk (which belonged to one of my sisters) on his knees. A man who was sweeping the road asked him what he thought he was doing and he said, "I thought I'd give Jinny a rest."

They had a kind neighbour who used to cook puddings for them and he in turn fetched bread for them from Fittleworth. One weekend they annoyed her over something so she never cooked their puddings. Next day she called at the bungalow for her bread and Chaus, as he was called, said "Hmmm no puddin' no bread."

Years ago father tells me there was a family lived at Wakestone whose daughter had married and lived not far away. She fell on hard times and her mother used to bake pies and cakes for her. Her father didn't approve of it so the mother did it on the quiet. One day having made a lot she thought of a plan to pretend a burglar broke in and took it all. So when she called a policeman in he soon rumbled it and said someone had broken out! Poor old dear it was very sad for her I'm sure. It's always so difficult where to draw a line about helping ones children and grandchildren.

I can remember a family living there when I was a schoolgirl and their grown up son used to go off to the "Diggers"[63] and get too much to drink and would come home and be sick all over the kitchen floor so his mother begged of him to have a bucket in there. This he did but kicked it over before going up to bed. It seems there was an awful lot of beer etc drunk in those days for I can remember my father telling me that he and another man took a job to cut a field of corn and they said they must have some drink so three barrels of beer was produced and they sat down and drank the lot before they struck a stroke as he says they worked like blacks on tea.

That reminds me of a man my father knew who always picked the

---

[63] the Well Diggers at Egdean

young shoots of blackthorn and let it wither down a little then scalded and drank it as tea. I tried it a few years ago but it was so colourless and very rough on the tongue. Poor old man he must have been poor and I can only repeat how much more fortunate people are today. How some of them suffered doesn't bear thinking about and as I've said before they hated the workhouse. I can just remember the one by the Masons Arms[64] at Petworth. My Grandfather Elliott spent quite a lot of time there until he came to live with my parents when I was very small. I think he came to live with them when the 5/- a week pension started.[65] I can remember when he signed his pension book for he had a mass of white hair and he always dried his pen on his hair which fascinated me very much. He didn't mind the workhouse as some people did for he used to be sent up to Petworth with a large basket to do shopping for the matron and he often had tobacco given to him by people who knew him. One day though somebody reported he'd been seen in a pub and that was the end of his shopping career.

Of course he used to work rough and sleep rough too. The older he got the less time he spent with his wife. Once he was looking after some animals (bullocks I think) on some low lying meadows around Arundel and sleeping in an old shed place with a loft over the top. It was very bad weather, nothing but rain, and one day the animals got on a dry piece of ground which was surrounded by flood water and grandfather was very worried about them and waded out waist deep to drive them to a safer place, after which he returned to the old shed which was cold and wet. He had no other clothes and had to stay all night as he was. My father said he was very foolish for had he gone to the farmer he would, he was sure, let him change his clothes and dry out. After that he got hip trouble and got very bent over.

---

[64] North Street, Petworth now the Stonemasons Arms
[65] Old Age Pensions Act 1908 introduced a pension of 5/- per week for people over 70 with income of less than £21 per year

He died when I was seventeen[66] and I can remember how he used to sit in the old armchair with his arms folded and in summer flying ants would come out of the brickwork and settle all over him and give us children (especially me) the jitters and when I said, "Oh Grandfather look at the ants all over you." He'd say, "That'll be all right my gal, they'll go back presently." And they did.

When we were older and had to go to work and return for holidays he always made a great fuss of us and on leaving would say, "Give me a kiss. Trust in the Lord and God speed the Plough and keep your bowels open."

Lillian's Grandfather, George Elliott senior, outside Mants.

He was very dear to me and when he was dying I was away from home and he told my mother to tell me not to tut for him. I can weep over it now. When we had a sing song party as we did a lot in those days he'd have a lot of drink before he'd look at my father and say "I never had my rights did I George. You know what I mean don't ye." And George would nod his head. I was very puzzled but understand quite well now of course.

---

[66] George Elliott Snr died 4th September 1923 aged 88

While he was at the workhouse grandfather said they had what was called a casual ward for tramps and various people who wanted a night's doss as they used to say. If they couldn't pay the men had to break stones before being allowed to leave, and the women had to do some washing. My grandfather used to put them in the way of doing it.[67]

There was another old man who lived at Fittleworth and the Relieving Officer of the district was always trying to make him go in to the workhouse. One day he threatened he'd tie a rope round him and drag him off but the old man said "You try and see" never dreaming he would. One day the Relieving Officer[68] arrived and the old man was in the Swan Hotel[69] having at drink. The Relieving Officer walked in and started putting a rope round the old man. Did he see red. He fixed hold of the Relieving Officer and dragged him to the other side of the road where there's quite a deep stream of water and pushed him in and sat on him. If another man who watched the scene hadn't persuaded the old man to get off and also told the Relieving Officer he'd asked for it and to get up and clear out, the old boy would have finished him, and who could blame him.

My father loves telling me about when he was a boy and there was a pub called the Fox Inn[70] which was finished before I can remember, all because someone made mischief telling a tale that drink was sold to people who were drunk on the premises. My father and grandfather were there at the time and another unfortunate old man who hadn't had much to drink but was bad on his pins.[71] First the policeman asked my father about grandfather who was very tired being working hard all day

---

[67] show them the work : JG
[68] an officer appointed by a parish to administer relief to the poor : OED. The Relieving Officer in the 1890's was John Lawrence
[69] The Swan at Fittleworth
[70] on the present A272 near the Bedham turning
[71] legs : Partridge

37

and had only just got in there and sat dozing. He soon jerked up when spoken to and then they tackled the old man and he had to get up and walk out and he fell down the steps. I think the local people thoroughly enjoyed themselves there for years.

A most amusing story he told me about a woman living quite near who had made a rabbit pudding and veg in a great pot over an open fire. She was waiting for her men folk to come home. One came home and said her husband had called in the Fox Inn. After a while the son said he'd go and fetch him out. When the lodger came home and the men hadn't arrived he said he'd go along and "fetch 'em out of it." This went on and none of them came in, so the woman got sick of waiting, off she went to the Pub and left the supper untouched. The others soon smoothed her over with a few drinks and it wasn't long before they were all singing high.

I suppose people really did have a rollicking time at the Pub, for there was an old girl who used to get in there and she'd drink and sing and one night she sat in there with a bottle of gin on her lap and singing high and rocking herself to and fro. Bye and bye she drank so much that she leaked on to the floor then down went her bottle of gin and broke, got mixed up with the water on the floor and a man who would drink just anything said, "Dang, Missus if I can see all that gin wasted." and laid down on the floor and lapped it up.

My father told me one day about a man who used to say he made 40 gallons of beer with two gallons of malt and this is what he made

> 10 gallons of strong beer
> 10 gallons of Robin Hood
> 10 gallons not quite so good
> 10 gallons of Twiny Twink

Another old man who worked at a farmhouse used to say that the farmer was brewing up some 18 horse power beer, 17 horses fetching the water while the 18th ran away with the malt. My father tasted Public house beer not so long ago and said "it's only fermented canal juice."

He is always telling me about how men (young ones) worked in farmhouses living in, sort of all round men he says. Their wages were very low but they were fed well. He said they often saved quite a lot of money. They were fed well eating lots of fat port and drinking a lot of home brewed beer or cider. Lots of people would shudder to look at all the fat meat now I tell him, and not so long ago I read that it was thought too much fat caused coronary thrombosis.

Nobody has eaten more fat meat than my father during his life time. He is a great believer in both fat and lean meat. Years ago he went to a butcher in Petworth on Saturday night and bought 5lbs of solid fat meat which had been taken from a prize bull he was told. It cost him a shilling and he got my mother to cook it and while it was cooling off on his living room table the man opposite, who was the father of the jolly boys I have previously mentioned, asked my father what he was going to do with that lot of fat and he said "Eat it. What do ye think I'm going to do with it but eat it?" The man turned away with a shudder. I'm afraid I would have done too for when I was a child I used to chuck it out of the window when father wasn't looking, as did my sisters. He says ice creams are what's bad for people. "Never tasted one in his life and don't want to." He loves saying people eat far to much old muck and spend too much time at the doctors and always taking too many tablets. I have to laugh for he thinks of doctors as "dead men makers."

Fat pork was used a lot in my grandmother's time. One of my father's favourite dishes was "Scrap Pie" made with squares of fat scraps that all the lard had been taken from. It must have been done in the old brick oven. The pie was made with a layer of scraps, a layer of apple sliced, a layer of currants and sultanas etc. Repeated 'till the pie dish was full and slowly baked.

My Grandfather Elliott once killed a pig weighing 70 stone and they had an awful lot of fat pork. People in those days were obliged to be self supporting and my father as a boy never knew what it was like to have a bit of butcher's meat unless he went to Mrs. Juggy Remnant at Potters.

When he tells me what sort of Christmas he used to have it opened my eyes, the difference in his childhood and the children of today. He said all he had was a piece of plum pudding and an extra glass or two of wine which more often than not he and his mother had by themselves. It didn't worry him for he never knew there was anything more to Xmas than that as far as presents were concerned.

I think by what I gather from him that it was the late Queen Victoria who started it all going, Xmas trees and so on. Yet he and mother did all they could to make Xmas a wonderful affair for us, my sisters and brother. Great excitement there was. On Xmas Eve my mother would go off to Petworth (walking of course, my father says we can't walk now, we've all got Petrol feet) and we children would sit all round the fire with our father and sing, not carols it had to be songs, and one particular song he was bent on us learning for some reason or other was the 'Charge of the Light Brigade'. The times we had to go over that I still remember to this day and I can see us now in my mind's eye making a half circle around the old log fire in the chimney corner. No other light most likely until our mother returned. We all hung our stockings up on the chimney wall with our names pinned on them.

Our parents went to a lot of trouble to make Father Xmas real even spreading the ashes around and making footprints on them. I well remember the Xmas when our parents couldn't get any thing in World War I and kept telling us not to hang our stockings up but we wouldn't believe them and oh the blow in the morning when our stockings hung limp and lifeless.

Our childhood days often reminds me of some verses I learnt at Bedham school at few lines of which go like this

> 'And fair young faces all ablush,
> Perhaps you may have seen some day,
> Roses crowding in the self same way
> Out of a wilding wayside bush'

I wish I knew who wrote those verses I know them all quite well.[72]

Its funny how various things in the local papers make my father recall things that he has been told by Grandfather Whitington. When, as mentioned before, he was working out under the downs he broke his leg and in those days they were taken back to the Parish where they were born and brought up.[73] He had a dreadful journey and was a long time getting about again.

When he eventually got alright he couldn't get any work and one day he decided to go to a fortune teller, she lived at Dunsfold. Before he reached this decision he had got very depressed because of no work and also someone had stolen a hive of bees. He lived at Crouchams, Kirdford so hadn't far to walk to Dunsfold. When he got to the lady's house he found that a lot of people were there already, they had left their carts along the lane. The fortune teller was very busy indeed. So my great grandfather sat down on a bank a distance down the lane and waited. Bye and Bye a voice called out "Ye can come in now master." And he hadn't a clue how she could have known he was there. She said "Let me eat my bit o' grub first and feed my cats." She had three lovely cats sitting by the fire. When that was done she started dealing

---

[72] An Order for a Picture by American Poet Alice Cary (1820-1871)
[73] See Appendix 3 – John Whitington and a broken leg

her cards about and presently she said "I see you are out of work master but don't worry ye'll have some before ye gets home I see." She said "You have lost a straw of bees.[74] For 5/- I will tell ye who took 'em and I could show ye a mirror and ye can see who took 'em." My great grandfather couldn't afford the 5/- so he had to leave it but she told him pretty clearly who it was. On the way home he met a farmer who said "Well Whitington I hear you are out of work. I want a man to do some ploughing. If ye like ye can make a start in the morning." This he did and during the day he went into a bit of a copse or Rue,[75] as my father calls it, to do a job for himself. On looking up in the trees there was his straw of bees, dead of course.

My father knows some very amusing stories which are rather spooky. I often wonder whether he believes in witchcraft. He was telling me one day about a young man who was working on a farm and he was feeling a bit sorry for himself as he had to go dung spreading. He said if the devil could catch him before he got over the field gate he could have him if only he'd do the dung spreading. He ran to the gate and was half way over it when he saw the dung flying about and the devil made a grab for him but the young man said, "Oh no, no halves."

Another story was about a man who had to thrash a lot of corn with a flail[76] (by hand) and he got terribly tired at the job. One morning he had a great surprise for he found a lot of the corn had been thrashed which he knew he hadn't done. He was very puzzled about it so the next night he decided to creep to the barn and find out what was going on. As he got near to the barn he heard little voices saying "You tweat I tweat" they were working so hard. The old man broke out "the devel tweat ye all or ye wouldn't be here." The little people never did any more of his thrashing.

---

[74] another name for a skep : JG
[75] 'a rough hedge and ditch division between fields' : DSD
[76] an instrument for threshing corn by hand : OED

There was a small boy round about that time who was helping a farmer as boys do sometimes and as he'd worked quite hard, the farmer gave him a penny. The boy put it on a ledge and said "I'll leave ye there till tomorrer." Next day the farmer changed it to a 2/- piece and the boy had a great surprise and said "You do look white, still I'll leave ye there til tomorrer." Next time the farmer changed it for sixpence. Next time the boy saw it he said "Coo ain't ye got white and thin. I'll leave ye there one more day." Next day the farmer changed it to half a sovereign and when the boy came round he said, "My ain't yer shrunk and now you're got Yeller jaundice I'd best put ye in my pocket fore ye gets any worse."

Years ago my father says a couple of men were discussing rabbits and one man said "Ye wants to go up over the downs to see big rabbits. I sin 'em up there as big as donkeys."
"What's the use of you talking like that" the other man said, "How could they get in their holes?"
"Ah" said the first man, "that be their business."

One old man that I can remember used to visit my parents and he lived in a van and half his time he never took his clothes off to sleep or anything – wore it till he wore it out, then got a new lot. One day when he called on my people he said he'd got a bad toe and my father was quite concerned and asked him questions – what was it like, what had he done to it and so on. Well he didn't really know so, by much persuading, he consented to take his sock off and let my parents have a look at it. In between his toes was a back collar stud. They removed it and the old man's toe was cured. Did my mother have a good laugh. She just couldn't help it. He didn't mind for he thought a lot of my mother as she did some shopping for him and after the collar stud lark she persuaded him to let her wash his underwear. He used to hire a taxi and take them out for the day sometimes and it gave them great pleasure as well as him I'm sure.

My father worked with a man once who made up his mind to save enough money to buy himself a new watch. Watches weren't very expensive in those days but their wages were very low. Anyhow this man bought a 2lb tin of corned beef which cost him tenpence. They were working away from home my father and this man and several others, probably haying or harvesting. He bought bread and that's all, no tea or sugar. The others used to make their tea in a billy can and put the eggs, if they had any, to cook for breakfast in the same lot of water. I have to smile at this, for I was always brought up to believe if you drank egg water it would give you scurvy. Anyway the tea was put in and when the other men had finished with it the man saving for the watch would have what was left. Towards the end of the week the corned beef being practically finished he eked it out by pouring tea into the tin and drinking that. On Saturday he bought his watch.

One man he worked with who bought a little joint used to scrape the oily fat off it with his knife and spread that on his bread the first day or two to make it last.

The year I was born, 1906, found my father with several other men tree felling and rinding at Haslemere. It was a miserable wet spring like the one just gone past and they lodged at a pub called the White Hart. The people were very kind to them. When they were looking for digs they met a man going to his allotment and asked him if he could tell them of any likely place and he said "You go along to the White Hart they might put you up." When they got there they found he'd played a joke on them for it was his wife and she laughed you bet.

Around the same spot a man was found dead under some laurels he'd been there about a year he heard, had come up from the coast. Like all those things it caused quite a sensation.

My father and his mates used to have a joint of meat between them and the landlady used to cook it for them. First half of the week my father let the ones get on with it that liked the outside best, nice and crisp but by Thursday the one who did the shopping said, "I'm tired of that meat, think I'll have bread and jam." The others would say the same and George used to get on with the meat, nice and red and sweet as a nut, he loves to say.

That job makes me think of all sorts of tales my father told me, one that somebody had cut loads and loads of Holly wood up but nobody would have it because its supposed to be unlucky to burn Holly wood. My father won't have it on his fire and if by chance I, or my sister, collect any by mistake he turns it out or gives to his neighbour who doesn't believe in such rubbish.

When my father and his mates were working at Haslemere they used to walk home on Saturdays and back on Sundays and think nothing of it. My mother used to meet him in Petworth and then they'd do their shopping and adjourn to the Wheat Sheaf at North Street. Meet their friends and have what he calls a jollification, then walk home to Bedham.

Makes me think of the story he told me of when one of my sisters was born. He was working for the people farming Bedham Manor[77] at the time and it was Goodwood Cup day and the farmer and his wife went leaving George in charge more or less. They had quite a large family but some were quite big children and they also left a cripple woman in charge to superintend their meals etc. While this was going on George Elliott was in a clam[78] because he wanted to be in two places at once. At home they needed some new china as it is with all families it soon gets broken. He decided to say nothing for he felt he must get the cups etc. as they were having a woman in to my mother's confinement, until the baby was born at any rate. So my father rushed off the Petworth as hard as his legs could go he tells me, got the china and tore back over

---

[77] John Purser farmed Bedham Manor at this time
[78] 'a cold sweat' : DSD – very anxious

45

Bognor Common with his bag dangling off his walking stick when 'wham' down it went on the ground and smashed the lot. He says he never felt so desperate as he did that day over babies but he cheered up when he arrived home for the baby had arrived and the woman gone home so they could make do with the china they'd got. Off he sprinted back to the farm and his work in the field near the house.

He had a lovely few months working for those people at the farm. He was young and jolly and when there was snow he'd snowball with the girls every chance he got and they were all jolly good at finding him drink when it was hot weather. I think he obliged the farmer whenever he got a chance. The farmer's wife he said was a wonderful worker. He has wonderful memories of the place and so have I for when I was a child I'd be up there with other children every time we could get away from chores of wood fetching, laundry etc. We used to play hide and seek in the summer moonlight and the farmers (different ones but old) never minded at all. The hens all ran wild there in my childhood and one thing gave me a great thrill. Seeing one of the hens walk proudly in with her family of yellow chicks, the farmer's wife had a lovely surprise.

It's amazing what a variety of jobs my father seemed to have. One job he did my mother hated and that was buying a piece of underwood[79] and cut out hoops[80] of all lengths, which I don't think is used today, and faggots,[81] bean sticks and Pea boughs etc. We used to work hard in the summer holidays carrying a lot of it out to a road for my father to deliver to villages around. My mother hated it because it meant she had to wait weeks for money sometimes with only her laundry money to lean on. It was a novelty at first going to the copse with our

---

[79] small trees or shrubs, coppice wood or brush wood growing beneath higher timber trees : OED

[80] a circle of wood for binding together the staves of casks or barrels : OED

[81] bundles of sticks, twigs or small branches… bound together – for use as fuel : OED

sandwiches but it soon grew tiring but we had to stick. I remember we once found a nightjar's nest with two babies almost ready for flight, the only ones I've ever seen.

One job I've omitted to say my father had was at a local Brick Kilns. It isn't used any more and the Kiln is turned into a dwelling house. The owner of the Brick Works[82] was a queer man, many said he was a Wizard. My father had queer ideas of him while working there for he always knew when their wagon load of faggots (for burning) turned over. All sorts of catastrophes happened while he and the old man's son went out with their loads whether it was near home or miles away.

Another amusing thing I remember about Brick Kiln Common was a man who lived in one of the cottages there who was a bit of a farmer, I say a bit because he wasn't a very good one, used to have too many irons in the fire as my father calls it and never really finished any jobs properly. Anyway when cars began to get a bit cheaper he bought a second hand one and built his garage round it and when finished he had made the doors too small to get the car out. It was never taken out just stayed and rusted away. My father also remembers a man who built a market cart for himself, made it big and strong, did it all in his shed and when finished he'd only an ordinary single door to get it out of the shed. Poor man he did cause some amusement.

A picture in the Southern Weekly last week took my father back years and that was hop-picking in 1900. He used to go when my elder sisters were children and he and my mother, like the Londoners, made a holiday of it, but he couldn't get on and work as he ought for the fun he was getting out of the Londoners and so on around. It gave him a great thrill talking and listening to them. He says they were paid every night so much, just holding enough back for their fares home I imagine. He says that's how everybody should be paid but I say it would cause a lot of trouble and trades people wouldn't get their money. But he

---

[82] The Brick Works at Brick Kiln Common was run by the Thayre family

47

maintains people wouldn't tick up[83] for things if they could pay every day.

I often think about the bad old days and the saying 'those were the days', I think as my father says "it's wonderful that old people can be independent with their pensions" but when I think my mother used to send us to Petworth to shop we'd get 3 pieces of beef from the butcher and 1 of suet which made a beef steak pudding enough for 6 or 7 of us and then some left. My mother used to warm it up for breakfast in a large frying pan and I can see her sitting over the open fire with the pan in one hand and a knife in the other gently lifting it so that it all got warmed up. It used to go down a treat.

Another thing I used to enjoy was when my mother had made some Parsnip beer with sliced parsnip and malt boiled in her copper furnace which the Estate put in for her when the Agent saw her struggling to boil clothes white in a black Pot, it held a bushel of water.[84] Its still in the garden but the bottom has fallen out of it. When I got in from school very hungry and I could smell the malt and slices of parsnip I used to have a good feed of it. Children were glad enough to eat anything in those days.

Thinking about food reminds me of a man my father knew who had a large family but said they never had an empty cupboard for one of the kids always had their heads poked in there looking for something. It's wonderful what tales he has to tell even about food. He can tell some tall stories believe me. One night a man arrived home from work and found no tea ready. He heard a groaning noise at the back of his cottage, went round and found his wife who said she was very sorry no tea was ready but she'd dug up such a big potato that she couldn't get it indoors.

---

[83] buy on credit : Brewers
[84] 8 gallons : OED

Mants – taken in the 1920's during repairs to the roof.

49

My father said he knew a gang of men who went away to work, got lodgings and had to pay 8/- per week all found. The first meal that was dished up to them was a regular feast. Roast beef, veg, suet pudding etc. The Landlord sat at the head of the table and when everybody was seated and ready to begin he said, "Now you chaps get on and eat as much as you like, when I button my waistcoat up you won't get any more."

I have never mentioned my father working at the River. Every so often to use his own words (I don't know if it's still done) the River Arun used to be cleaned out. When the water was very low of course. Apparently the farmers in those days used to do the paying indirectly for an incident happened to prove it. At one time a gang of men was employed there who thought they'd have a lovely time in between whiles. My father wasn't there that year but he heard about it. Some of the men were keen on fishing and would waste their employer's time doing just that till their boss came along and found them at it. One of the farmer's daughters had been having a look round with Binoculars on and it was explained to them. I think they were all dismissed. This farmer's daughter used to spend a good bit of her time spying on the farm workers as well and one day a man thought he'd teach her a lesson. So he got into a corner of a field quite a distance away slipped his trousers down and turned round so that she could have a good view of him bending over. She didn't do it again.

One year my father took a job as ganger to clean the River at Pallingham and he had the bright idea of filling all the holes in the sides of the river banks instead of chucking it on the top. When the boss came round he was very angry and said it looked as though they hadn't done any work. Had he seen a nice lot of mud on the top of the banks all would have been well. After much discussion my father agreed to do as the boss said and the next time he came round he was delighted with what they'd done.

When my father was a boy he said there was a gentleman farmer who farmed Pallingham[85] and did it wonderfully well and he was a very good man to work for too. People stayed on his farm for years until he died in fact. He had a friend at Hawkhurst and they used to talk to each other from their homes with Bugles. People around got used to it and understood that some kind of message was passing between them. Once when the man from Hawkhurst visited Pallingham he was astonished to see great lumps of clay spread about his meadows and said to his friend, "My dear John what do you mean by having all this clay on your meadows?" and he said "You wait and see when spring comes and my men get the harrows going and breaking and spreading it." And the other man saw a wonderful crop of grass. Clay was dug out of the ditches all round the farm and it's a wonderful fertiliser, my father tells me. He also says that people are silly to neglect their hedges and ditches as they do today. Its bad farming he says.

I tell him all I can about things I see daily and he wags his head and thinks people are mad or lazy. Two men he remembers spent all their lives with the farmer mentioned above at Pallingham. One had two thumbs on one hand. Both of these men lived in I believe. They were broken hearted when the old farmer died and they had to find fresh homes. One was a great hunk of a chap, a bit simple in some ways. I can just remember him in a smock.[86] He finished up at the top of Bedham. The last few years of his life he used to live with a relative and she was a very hard worker outside and at home, so he used to stay in bed all winter and get up when spring came. He used to work with the horses on the farm and when haying was on the go he'd lead the horse as the hay was loaded. He got very bored with the job and after a time he'd say, "Dass it all, keep 'Olloin stand fast 'ittle ways makes my head bad Hm m m."

---

[85] John Mellersh who farmed at Pallingham from at least 1851 to 1876
[86] a loose-fitting garment of coarse linen or the like, worn by farm labourers over or instead of a coat and usually reaching to mid-leg or lower : OED

51

He used to be a great Joke with the other men. He was as strong as a horse and could carry a sack of wheat from one end of the farm to the other. Often when sowing wheat this happened with the encouragement that on the way to the Granary where wheat was kept he was told "Call and get yourself a drink of cider."

My father recalls a story he heard years ago about a gentleman who lived at Barkfold House. He was a the parish councillor; each parish in those days had their own council. Although there were no unions in those days men used to put their heads together and demand a rise sometimes. At this particular time they made up their minds they wanted another shilling a week and the leaders went round to as many men as they could for support. One man they went to on a farm said, "I can't do that, Masser give me the sack." They said, "Sack or no sack, you've got to come."

They all went to the meeting at which I gather the gentleman at Barkford presided. He had arrived in his carriage and the men demanded their rise and he said, "No they couldn't have it." So the spokesman said, "If you don't agree we'll drag your carriage an' all down to the river an' push you in." He didn't believe them but they fixed him and dragged the carriage without any horses and off they went. Got right to the bridge and were just ready to push the carriage over when he gave in to pay up.

My father tells me that when tractors first came into being on some farms the carters hated the idea as did the men who cut the grass with scythes; for he can remember when a farmer said he was having his grass cut with a machine and horses, some men drove artines (I doubt if that's spelt correctly)[87] all over the fields to break the knives on the

---

[87] the comment in brackets is Lillian's own. To date no explanation has been found for 'artines' however the OED defines tines as "a series of projecting sharp points on some weapon or implement, as a harrow, fork, eel spear etc" and from the context it is likely that spikes were hidden in grass

mowing machine but break or no break, the mowing machines won the day.

I do feel that people were much jollier in those days and there always seemed one clown on the farm to entertain everybody and even the farmers enjoyed them. One man my father knew was a jolly good worker but bad at getting up in the morning. If the farmer chastised him about it he'd say "ye want me 'ere fore I gets up then?" When they were extra busy once the farmer knew this chap, who was a bachelor, wanted to go to the local fair. He begged of him not to but no good, off he went and the next morning he creeps in with his bed clothes on feeling very poor he had had too much beer. The farmer said "for God's sake Neddy pull your socks up and get on with your work."
He said "You'll 'ave to give me some cider first then." And he soon recovered himself.

Someone once saw him outside a butcher's shop and he was busy wolfing down sausages raw. When asked if he couldn't wait to get them cooked he said "What I fancies my guts 'as to put up with."
One day he had too much to drink and wandered off into a churchyard near by his pub and laid down. A policeman saw something lying on the grass and went over to him, shook him up and said "Come on out of it. You're not allowed to do this." He pulled himself up right and said "Why don't ye gorn rouse them other up down there they bin there longer 'n I have." So the policeman walked off down the path to have a look round and Neddy jolly soon hopped it.

Sometimes I regret trying to do this at all for I'm sure my father has lots of visitors and I'm pretty certain he tells a good many of them the same as he tells me. Why I think that is because sometime ago I was staying with my daughter and there was a film or story on telly built up round a tale my father has told me many a time about a man who, when a boy, climbed a tree and on getting down slipped and hung by one foot. He yelled for help which did eventually come and he always had to walk with a limp. When grown up he wore a beard and old Peak cap and used to get into a Pub at Kirdford telling notorious lies of how he'd been to sea and been shipwrecked, swum to shore hangin' on to a plank. It just rolled off his tongue for he had a wonderful imagination. But also one day my father and his neighbour went in the pub and just heard the end of one of his stories, of course they both laughed outright and the other men who'd been listening wanted to know what they were laughing about. Then they blowed his gaff as they say and that put pay to the free beer he'd been getting.

It is now potato planting time and its recalls to my father of how when a young man he and another were employed potato digging and my father bet his mate he could eat a gallon of potatoes at one meal when new. His mate bet him a shilling he couldn't. The spuds were cooked in due course and brought out and my father got down to the last three and his mate said "I'll be dammed if you shall have them I can see I've lost."
My father says his mother could eat a gallon of new spuds as he call them without any trouble, but yet he says she suffered with indigestion a lot. I don't wonder.

I'm always interested in various remedies that he thinks of, which people used to use. It came across his mind one day that a man he knew used to go down to the river at this time of year to pick 'bog beans' which I gather were the young shoots of a plant. He used to take them home and scald them and drink the water for liver trouble. He knew people who used to collect droppings of sheep and soak them in cider and drink for jaundice.

A Huntsman on the Leconfield Estate years ago was riding around Brick Kiln Common passed a cottage and saw a sick boy there and asked the mother what was the matter with him. She said "Whoopin' cough but doctor can't do nothin' for him." The huntsman said "Got any snails around the house? Must have ones that are sealed. Get a needle and prick through the back of the shell and hold it over a teaspoon of sugar. Give him some everyday." This she did and in a few days the boy had greatly improved and when the doctor called again he was very surprised and she told him what had happened. She was so pleased and the doctor said it was more than he could do.

My Grandmother Elliott, so I thought was a great ointment maker but it was one of her neighbours. She used to make White Rose ointment and ointment made with the flower called 'Heal All.'[88]

When my father was a boy he chopped the top of his thumb off and it got very septic and painful. A swelling came up under his arm and he couldn't sleep at night. Someone advised him to go to a lady at the top of the hill and he always wished he could remember the stuff this lady made into a poultice. He can remember scrapings of some kind of soap and I think brown sugar also the fine scrapings of a horn tooth comb as he calls it.[89] He had to go every day for several weeks.

When I and my sisters were children we had to have old fashioned remedies too, snails juice for whooping cough, cider sop for measles. The idea of cider brought to the boil and poured over the broken up bread and eaten as warm as possible was to bring the spots out. It did the trick too. I was horrified for days over my spots but when they faded away we were allowed to get up. I can also remember when we were running about in a very spotty condition a man came to do some repairs to the house and he scolded my mother for not keeping us in bed until the spots had disappeared. I only remember seeing a doctor in our home twice, once for my father and sister and once for my brother. Sister had come home from work with Spanish Flu.[90] Father

---

[88] probably Common Valerian (valeriana officinalis)
[89] a comb carved from cattle horn – often oxen
[90] the Spanish Flu Pandemic, also known as the 1918 Flu Epidemic, killed some 25 million to 40 million people worldwide in 1918 - 1919

got it then I and my brother and sister. No doctor for us and were we ill. How we survived God alone knows. My mother and grandfather kept themselves immune by sipping gin all the time we were infectious. Grandfather took off to the Well Diggers for it and each time my Mother attended us she rinsed her mouth out with gin. For weeks after my mother used to get us up and in a little while it would be "Mum can I go back to bed?" It was awful.

My brother had an accident when he was eight years of age. We all used to be very expert at walking on stilts but it came to a sad end one night when, on a damp evening my brother went off round the house on his stilts, struck out and landed on father's newly trimmed hedge, a piece of which entered his trouser and came through his flesh in a very serious place, but father lifted him very carefully and carried him indoors. My mother nearly 'done her nut' as they say these days. I and an older sister walked all the way to Pulborough[91] for a doctor. Did sister get chewed up[92] for dragging little me with her at that time of night. I think it was late summer. By the grace of God no serious damage was done but my brother walked with two sticks for quite a while.

There happened to be a friend of one of my sister's staying with us that summer who entertained my father with her stories of poaching days with her father. She came from Surrey but the piece which took the cake was when she sat up in the chimney corner one night and said "Ye know Mr. Elliott (she directed most of her conversations to my father my mother not being a very talkative person) I always made up my mind that I'd never get married till I met someone perfect, then I met my Will and he was perfect so I married him of course." It used to tickle me pink.

As a child I was an awful mimic and poked fun at everybody. If my

---

[91] approximately 6 miles
[92] told off : JG

mother took me to a jumble sale (she used to go to a lot and buy things to renovate into clothes for use and my father always encouraged her to buy men's clothes which he got great fun out of selling to his mates) I'd look at all the ladies grovelling over all the stalls and stored up all the funny things and faces in my mind and dish them all to my father when I got home. He must have encouraged me into it or I wouldn't have done it. I expect children are having their go at me now.

A favourite saying of my father's to us as children used to be "You mustn't poke fun of the foolish, you might be struck comical yourself one day." I went baby sitting for my daughter a while ago and the wee son, aged a year, wouldn't settle down whatever I did to console him so his sister, aged seven and a half, leaned over from her bed towards me and peering through his cot said "I expect he thinks you're an horrible old lady Nanny." That shook me badly but I tried not to show it. Too outspoken like her grandmother.

Martha Elliott nee Stevens with her daughter Alice and her son George.

I love being a grandmother although I got dreadfully upset when I was at the age of sixteen my mother was a granny for the first time. I remember I kept looking at her to see if she had aged and I know I dreaded my parents getting old and left alone. I wept bitterly when my brother, who is the youngest, got married and went off for his honeymoon and couldn't control myself. While he was there I hadn't worried and when my mother died I had a dreadful time. After the funeral one of my brothers-in-law followed my father to the chicken house and said

57

"You'll have to pack up now Dad." But Dad never answered. He didn't intend to move from Bedham I'm sure and the first winter 1946-47 several of us did shift days and he wasn't left but by spring '47 all but two of us had dropped out and the following September I had it to myself as regards staying nights.

Just over fifteen years I slept there two nights a week and of course the following days. Since then I have, as stated before, slept there most nights having to fight for the odd night off. Why I have mentioned this is because I'm always interested in that thing called love that one reads and hears so much about. I've long since decided that the people who have large families live for themselves and their own enjoyment and the children bring themselves up. They are rarely spoilt and when they in turn produce children mostly only one or two, they say to themselves, 'I'll see them have a better time than I did.' Result spoilt children and very unhappy grown ups they turn into and do they spoil their children, not on your life. So to me its all a vicious circle like everything is. My father and I have great arguments over these things. He had a lovely, happy married life he has told me no end of times and if he had his time over again he'd do just the same.

Talking of vicious circles to him, we both agree that in years to come rural England will be like it was so many centuries ago, a Ruler over each county. We are very puzzled over the way the common land which has always been governed by the big land owners, they having to pay for the manorial rights, seem to let every Dick, Tom and Harry fence in pieces of common left right an' centre. Its so different to what it was when I was a child and when my father was a boy. He remembers being told how a great fight went on over someone fencing in a piece of land, enormous sums of money were spent by both gentlemen in question fighting it out and the fence had to come down.[93]

The cottages at Bedham were built, so the story goes that has been

___

[93] 1882 The High Court Case of Nicholls v. Mitford

handed down, by charcoal burners in Tudor times. My father says that he was told that the settlers, as he called them, built the chimneys first and if smoke came up through the chimney by sunrise they could claim the place. They added on to it by degrees using old ship's timbers brought up by barges to Pallingham. Of course the cottages were improved a good deal when the settlers fell on hard times and they were bought out by a land owner who owned the cottages until World War I, after which they were sold in lots a little bit of land going with each of them.

When my father was a boy they had a very heavy snow one year with a blizzard blowing the snow up into the roofs and all the ceilings of the cottages fell down. I think it was 1881. All the little cottages then had a tiny trap door put into the bedroom so that the tenant could get up into the roof to sweep the snow out. But my father says it never happened again in his memory.[94]

Some of these cottages have changed hands several times. One of them used to be a shop years ago I'm told and my father was told by my Great Grandfather Whitington about the queer ways the shop owner had at times and this worried his son very much. He told my great grandfather all about it, how every few nights he would disappear for a while and after that he'd seem better for a few days. So my great grandfather advised the son to follow him one night. This he did and when he got down into the copse below the house his father turned off in the undergrowth and there was a great scuffling noise going on but the son was too scared to go and investigate because of annoying his father. After a while his father came out and mooched off home, the son hiding up until he'd gone. He thought his father had been fighting with the devil but my father has a quite different opinion. He thinks the shopkeeper had been linked up with some smugglers and they hid the goods in the copse.

---

[94] these trapdoors can still be seen in some of the cottages, including at Mants

Another family who lived there years ago behaved oddly. The woman stayed in bed for three months and then got up and went straight out into a copse pimp making.[95]

My father knew a man when he was very young who was always suspected of sheep stealing, in fact he really was a sheep stealer but the Authorities never could catch him out right. However he was ordered to clear out of the county. He went to Thorney Island and stayed there for twenty years after which he was a free man again. Some time after he returned to Bedham district he went squirrel hunting with some boys/lads and in a certain place in a wood below where my father lives this man climbed a tree and after looking for a squirrel he jumped down out of the tree and said "Dammed if this ground don't sim holler to me, must be somethin' buried here."
So they raked and dug about with sticks and found a tub sealed up full of mutton which had been pickled in salt for years and it was lovely my father was told. Of course the sheep stealer knew it was there all the time.

Which reminds me of another man who made his home under a big bush and dug and dug to make himself comfortable sort of mud armchairs cut into the earth. He spent 20 years there so my father says, only came out to go to shops etc. Eventually he was discovered by fox hounds and after that he was made to get out of it. I think he finished up in a workhouse. My father thinks he'd been let down by a woman and resolved to be a hermit. People say and do queer things but there's usually a motive behind it.

My father knew a man, when he was a boy, who always loitered about to be the last to move off when the Fox Inn closed at night and when somebody chipped him about it he said "I'd rather go home when owls holler than fools wander." But the general idea was that he was a poacher.

---

[95] a pimp is a 'small bundle of chopped wood for lighting fires' : DSD

One night years ago a man got lost in a wood somewhere around Storrington and he was scared stiff and kept shouting for help. An Owl answered 'oooohhh' and he said "Mr. Woods of Storrington give anybody 2d to see me on the right road" but all the owl said was 'ooooh'.

A man my father knew and worked with when he was a young man left the Pub at Stopham Bridge[96] one night with a gang of chaps, dodged over into the river meadow to do a job for himself, stepped into the water and, it being dark, lost his bearings and was afraid to move so hung to a tree there until day light. It must have been awful suspense for he'd had a son drowned some years before. This man's wife was ever so kind to my elder sisters, one being named after her. When they had measles and my mother had to go to Petworth she popped down with a jolly great rice pudding. Called up the stairs and told them not to come down they could have it when Mum got home. She hadn't got out of the gate when the most daring one hopped out of bed and down the stairs taking the pudding and some spoons. When Mum arrived home an empty dish greeted her on the kitchen table. Thinking about the milk pudding makes me think of the answer my father gave me when I said "I wish I could afford a refrigerator."
"You want it about as much as a toad wants a side pocket."

While writing this my husband is listening to a boxing contest and it reminds me that my Great Grandfather Whitington trained as a boxer at Storrington but his parents hated it so he gave it up. Always though he couldn't resist challenging people when having a drink in Pubs etc. Around this time there was another man who would go into a Pub and pick up anybody's pint of beer just to aggravate people and if they grumbled he would say "Come outside." One day this happened to Whitington and he agreed to go outside. The man knocked him down six times but the seventh he got knocked down and was given a good hiding and that finished him. He never picked up other people's beer

---

[96] the White Hart

after that. Whenever he came into a Pub after that some body would chaft him by saying "Old Clay legs[97] was one too many for ye, wasn't he."

My father was really educated by Clay legs for he could always defend himself. One day as a boy he was sent off to a place called Burdocks with a carpenter's bag full of eggs by his mother and someone gave him a ride in a cart and of course it smashed the lot, it was awful he said. Another time he went off to fetch shopping and a boy spilled it all but George got his knife out and slashed it across the boy's wrist. He was wearing irons at the time. He suffered a lot but it made him very courageous.

'Honour thy father', I wonder how many times over the last 17 years I have had cause to think of that, being torn this way and that on account of my husband's ill health and my efforts to let my father have his wish to stay in the old home he has stayed in for 85 years and, as now, with my husband convalescing after a few weeks in hospital. For weeks past I haven't had the ghost of a chance to do any writing. While my husband was in hospital at Chichester I had a very hectic time, although I was able to enjoy the quiet of Priory Park in between the visiting times. It was the strain of getting back to Bedham at night and the rush to get my father's chores done and leave everything before dashing off through the wood to catch the mid-day bus to Chichester. My husband is well enough to drive the van up there now and stay each night. I think he is quite happy about it. I'm always torn between my husband and my father as well as my grandchildren, who are very precious to me, but I cannot make their mother understand how impossible it is to split myself up any more than I do. I'm always looking around at other human beings young and middle aged and old and I find it jolly interesting and of course they look at me and criticise me for what they take as my neglect of my husband for my father. Even he has in years gone by. When I have criticised my sisters who won't spend a night or

---

[97] John Whitington's nickname

62

day with him he has quoted the piece out of the marriage service which goes something like this 'and cleave her (him) only unto you.'[98] I feel sometimes he hates my guts for being so dutiful to him. Yet he loves staying there.

All this reminds me of a doctor I worked for, for years who, when I was cooking his dinner would discuss his troubles with me and I'd say "Pack up and be done with it, I never believe we are intended to live in misery as you are doing."
"You should believe the vows you made in church" he'd say. I'd toss my notorious head and say "only man made laws." He would be very shocked indeed. Everything in life is so contradictory. One thing I did see on my wanderings at Chichester while my husband was in hospital that gave me food for thought and that was the very young people, very much in love going around hand in hand then the very aged doing just that. Does that mean when a couple has got old they suddenly become very precious to each other again? I'm sure it had nothing to do with the traffic. I think all those days dodging around Chichester did me good mentally. One gets into an awful rut hanging around home or homes, doing nothing but cleaning, cooking etc.

My husband loves doing the gardening and only wished me to advise but when he is ill I have a dabble at it and it is very rewarding indeed. I hope I'll never turn into one of those people who cannot enjoy doing something for nothing. My father has always been like that I'm sure, and other Bedham people tend to be like that among the workers.

One often hears of women being the weaker sex but I'm dammed if I'll believe it although I often notice that with married couples there's always one donkey who does all the hard work, giving, loving and everything. I've seen it repeatedly. Often in this it's the man who does it all but quite often it is the woman. It's when neither wants to work, love and give that the marriage goes to the rocks. I'm sure it was my

---

[98] from the old Book of Common Prayer

63

mother who was the unselfish one, much as I love my father I know it as sure as God made little apples as they say. I, being half mother and half father find myself being the same but just now and then I kick over the traces before the doormat begins to wear out quite. I often feel I'd like to bury my head in the sand and forget everything and everybody then I pull myself together and remember the story I used to love at school 'King Bruce and the Spider.'

While I am working at my father's and my husband is sitting around my father is telling him all the old stories of his past and I feel more than a little sad because he doesn't seem to realise that I've heard them before. He was telling us a story this morning about a farmer who worked on a farm with his mother, father was dead. This man, who was one of a family who didn't like work but were all big eaters, made up his mind to get some money out of selling some bullocks and when he'd got the money he'd clutter off to Canada. He schemed up a plan to borrow money on the strength of these animals from a money lender. He hired a chap to be there when the money lender called and showed him the bullocks he wished to raise money on, then kept him talking while the man he hired drove them through a gap into another meadow, then took the money lender along to see them. The money lender gave him so much money there and then and that night he disappeared. During the next week the money lender sent for the animals but they belonged to the Farmer's mother and he couldn't do a thing about it as in those days people couldn't be found so easily.

We listen to the 8 o'clock news every morning at Bedham and always it seems there's been a robbery or an accident or a murder or something and my father says "it's no worse than it used to be years ago." This morning he told us a story his Grandfather Whitington told him about three Turnpike Sailors[99] as they were then called. Horrible lazy scamps who used to go about barefoot and get their living by hab-grab and

---

[99] "a beggar in the guise of a distressed sailor… also one who frequents the turnpike or turnpike road" : OED

cunningness he says. They went to a couple of cottages on Bognor Common and a young girl was alone in one of them. They killed her and washed their hands in River Hill stream and father says for years nobody could persuade horses to drink from the stream. The three men were captured and two of them turned King's evidence but the third wouldn't open his mouth so he was put between weights and was killed by the weights for he could never be made to speak.[100] I wonder how far back in history such a method of crushing weights goes?

After hearing of the Turnpike Sailors my father said he heard talk of a couple of chaps who were also on the scrounge some years ago at Strood Green. One went up to a cottage door and the other lingered half way up the path. When the woman who lived there opened the door she listened to the first man while looking at the second man. She spoke to the second one and the first said, "no use talkin' to him, Ma'am he's deaf and dumb." The woman said "Deaf and dumb! He never used to be and he'd better clear out before I have him cleared out." He was her own brother.

George Elliott aged 90.

My father hates the Radio but I'm afraid I make him put up with it in the mornings. I feel sure it does him good mentally and gives him food for thought and keeps his brain going. Whether his ideas are right or wrong I don't know but we've just heard of the terrible earthquake in Yugoslavia. My father ponders this over and then says, "Well we'd have them in this country for the foul air is in the ground here same as there, but our climate always being so wet it doesn't happen, you know."

---

[100] this was the last time the punishment of pressing (crushing) was used in England – see Appendix 4 Pressing or Peine forte et dure

He says "We get them Jack O'Lanterns in the very boggy places and years ago, over a hundred it is, some men dug a well for water at Hawkhurst which is now a school. They kept going down and had got to the depth of a hundred feet. Their boss had warned them not to go any further when they found winkles shells, but one man kept on digging and he was overcome by foul air and died. Another one at the top who held a lighted candle down over the hole had his beard burnt off one side of his face. When the dead man was got out they found winkle shells in his waistcoat pocket."

The Jack O'Lanterns, as my father calls them, are phosphorus lights which keep bobbing up and down and can be seen on a dark night. He doesn't advise anybody to follow them. He knew a man who did that years ago and he messed his pants because he got lost in the bogs and wandered about till daylight. People used to tease the man about it he says.

My husband is always interested in the way my father starts talking as soon as he gets up (my husband has his breakfast in bed) and goes on and on about different things which has happened in the past. I'm often intrigued about history repeating itself in one's lifetime, always depending on how long one lives I suppose. My father, after reading in the local Gazette how a youth had thrown himself into the Arun because of a girl, recalled to mind how a youth did just that years ago at Petworth Mill. We argue about it for he says they are weak minded people to let things get on top of them. I agree that no woman is worth killing oneself for, but they are very strong and brave to do such a thing. I think mostly they are people with an unhappy childhood. I often think I'm a queer creature myself, for why do I wait on my father and can't bear his life to be disturbed when we rarely agreed about anything? I have far more patience with him than with my own husband. One of my father's favourite sayings goes like this "I don't think you are like my mother for she used to say Patience and Water is the thing to have."

I've never mentioned the different people that used to find their way to Bedham during my father's childhood. Some going round with tracts which were religious papers. I gather one was very queer mentally and always came with his wife. She had a dreadful time with him it seems. She used to keep bees. The man got so bad they put a strait jacket on him my father says, and took him away. When he returned home he worked like mad for a while, then one day a bee stung his wife on her throat and she died. He went queer again and hung himself on an apple tree.

Another man came around selling boot laces. He was always swishing a pithy[101] stick in front of him and he was also queer for he told people he had walked up over Duncton Hill and saw a man walking in front of him along the Downs and then he suddenly disappeared. Some time afterwards the man with his boot laces was found in a pit over Duncton Hill dead. People said he had seen his ownself disappear, a sort of premonition, that's what I think my father means.

Bad omens have been discussed between us a lot lately. Its several months since I've had an opportunity to jot anything down during which time sad happenings have called forth bad omens between us. One night I was having tea with my husband in our own home when suddenly my husband looked very upset and said "What's the matter with that B.... Robin out there." I hadn't heard it being very bunged up with a cold. So I said "You don't believe in bad omens surely?" He wouldn't say anything so the matter was dropped. During the following week a sad thing happened to a young lad we both knew very well. I told my father about it and he said an old lady used to take notice of Robins if they kept on singing. She'd say "Hark at that Robin singing over my grave." Then he went on to say how when my grandfather was on his deathbed (I have mentioned him previously), he was very ill for a fortnight, and my father and mother and some of my

---

[101] a stick cut from wood that is still growing and full of pith (often elder), so strong and flexible - JG

sisters did all they could for him. One day my father says as he was sitting at the table with a glass of home made wine, he tipped it up and drank it, put the glass down on the table and it split with a sharp snick right up the side and he said "My father will be dead before tomorrow this time." and he was. They all stood round him and he said "well folk death is upon me, Farewell to ye all." and he was gone, just like that.

I heard my first ticking spider when my mother died. I told my brother and made him come and listen to it but he wouldn't say what he thought. Of course a lot of people say it is all Phooey but I don't know. It's like the witch craft for since this awful rain (it is now November 19th and raining every day) I told my father that the water was up at Tanners Brook and he says there should be plenty of room for it to get away for a man once saw a woman go under the Coker, as he calls it, riding her donkey and disappeared down the meadow. He ran for his life home to his people and was scared out of his wits. I wonder whether it is true and I wonder if the man who years ago kept the pub called the Bush at Plaistow really did shake half crowns out of his apple trees. He bet a man 5£[102] he could do it and the man lost his 5£. I asked my father whether it was supposed to have happened in his memory but he said not, though it wasn't long before, for his own mother knew the man her father often talked about it.

I think sometimes that there's either a ghost in the old tumbledown cottage where my father lives or else he does things to try and test me. I often find the door leading into the lean to shed bolted during the morning after I've opened it up and been through it quite a few times. I have a laugh with my father over these things and when I was shaken in my bed early one morning I jumped out and flashed my torch about and looked everywhere to see if a cat had got in. I called out to my father and he hadn't heard anything and told me in his grandfather's time they'd say I was 'Hag ridden', meaning an old witch had been

---

[102] Lillian always writes the £ sign after the number

sitting on my chest. Later in the day I heard about the earth tremor which affected West Sussex. I was so glad there was an answer to my queer sensation that a cat had leapt off, or, on my bed.

Still strange things are happening for one night since, I had just settled myself comfortably in bed with my library book when my father called out and asked if I could hear a chair moving in his room by the window. I shouted back that I thought he was doing something himself and he said "No, he was in bed" and would I get out and with my torch investigate.[103] This, with my heart in my mouth I did. I actually saw the chair move but didn't say so. I picked it up and banged it back down again then returned to bed. I didn't hear it again. I'm getting used to these queer things.

I was telling my father how cruel I think the laws are getting about people not being allowed to stay in their homes when they get old unless they have someone with them. I heard a story to that effect on the Radio and I think it's awful if, as this person did, she owned her own home. My father soon enlightened me that is nothing new, for he knew an old lady when he was a boy who moved to a wee cottage at Churchwood which was left by an endowment for old people.[104] The old lady was quite active but, when she hadn't been seen for a few days someone got a ladder and climbed up and looked in her bedroom and saw her sitting up in bed playing 'patience', reported it and she was removed to a workhouse. Poor old lady, what a dammed shame. I don't think I would go without a fight. We've all got to die some time and my mother begged to do just that when she got ill. I'm all for it too and that's why I look after my father as I do. We are all told there's no place like home yet as soon as the old people want waiting on their hearts are broken by being told they mustn't live alone.

---

[103] during George Elliott's tenancy of Mants the cottage had neither electricity nor mains water. He left Mants in 1963

[104] Lee's Charity at Fittleworth

Some weeks have gone by since I last put pen to paper and winter is upon us with our first severe frost and my father is feeling it pretty badly and I am struggling to keep the Ingle nook fire well supplied with wood. Kindling wood cannot be bought for money now, I have made enquiries and am told there's no call for faggots etc. What is there better than a lovely wood fire and I feel sure healthier.

I had my weekly night off last night from father's and in the morning I have to talk to him about various things concerning my sister who does night duty. I always use evaporated milk diluted and so does my sister. She loves finishing up what I've left and leaving me her small tin intact but I tell my father I'm like my mother used to be, independent. I prefer my own milk and don't like working "wheel within wheel'. It's been in my system for years as, when I was about 19 or 20, I worked as a cook in a beautiful old house. There were three of us, cook, parlourmaid and housemaid. The gardener who brought in the coal was in his 60's and for some reason I never knew, used to boss the show. I'd only been there a few weeks when he started putting his arms round my shoulders and trying to kiss me. I was horrified and told the Lady of the house I'd rather get the coal in myself and that was alright for a while, but he soon started coming his old tricks again. I wouldn't wear it, already having a tall, dark and handsome young man with a motor bike. Anyway I told the Lady and had to walk the carpet[105] where the gentleman of the house said, "You know Lily you won't get on in this world if you don't learn to work wheel within wheel."
"Well" I said "if wheel within wheel means letting the old gardener kiss me I've finished." So I gave a month's notice and they said, "You'd better go now."
So with a month's wages in hand, I packed up and went home to Bedham, to my parents' amusement I daresay.

These people I worked for were not husband and wife. She told the

---

[105] to be reprimanded, particularly "servants summoned to the parlour for a wigging: Partridge

story to me that down in Cornwall her husband had accidentally shot himself and when he was dying begged of Bill, whom she now lived with, to take care of her. The house had a secret staircase by a big fireplace in a gigantic lounge and we never knew when they went to bed, but in the morning the sweet little housemaid of 16 took their morning tea to them and of course went to the lady first. They had rooms opposite each other. She would call out "Morning Bill" and he would say "Morning Mollie" and Bill's dressing gown would be on Mollie's bed so the housemaid informed us.

The Parlourmaid and I got on very well but the Housemaid being Cornish used to go up to the old gardener's house when his wife was gone to shop.

My kitchen was huge and a long way from the rest of the house and in those days I loved singing and would open out as loud as I could. The parlourmaid told me I was called "The Local Choral Society." The lady and the gentleman used to be large whisky drinkers and the three of us staff used to share the 5/- given us for the returned empties monthly.

People laugh at us working class country bumpkins but by gad we could write volumes on what we've seen and heard after a few years domestic service. Of course I've read 'What the Butler Saw'[106] and 'The Indiscretions of a Lady's Maid',[107] and I loved them both.

I was very young to take a job of cooking like the one I've just mentioned but I worked for nearly six years for a sweet lady[108] who had a little adopted son whom I loved very much and looked after a lot and when he was in bed I used to watch a daily cook who came in and gradually I got to doing a three course meal myself. I had a flair

---

[106] by E.S. Turner (1962) reprinted by Penguin Classic History 2001
[107] by William Le Queux (1911)
[108] Mrs. Davies Colley at Daymans, Bedham

for it and used to study all the cookery books. I think cooking is like nursing and teaching etc, it's a gift and it grows on you to be good at these things, practice too makes perfection. Now, since my husband is always on a diet, I hate cooking and when one reads that people dig their graves with their teeth I'm inclined to agree and I do believe that so much cooking is quite unnecessary for you get the vitamins required in many other ways and so spare the digestion. Youngsters need a lot of food but once middle age is reached "some is plenty, enough is too much" should be the motto.

Thinking back over my working in different jobs makes me think of an elderly woman who worked as a Charlady as they were then called. We've gone up one now and are known as daily or home helps. This particular woman used to work where I did and loved, over our lunch, to tell stories of her days as a head parlourmaid and things they said. One lady she worked for in London used to frequently have a pudding on Sundays called "Prune Shape".[109] It was very nice and one Sunday there was a bit left and it was finished up in the Servants' Hall. That evening when pudding was taken in the parlourmaid finished her job and was just going out of the door when her Ladyship said "Will you bring the rest of the Prune Shape in Emma." Poor Emma looked very embarrassed and had to admit it was eaten. She was told to go from the room and scarcely had the door closed when the Lady said in a loud voice "Scavengers."

My first job at the age of fourteen nearly killed me. There were 8 maids kept and oh the poor little underlings like myself slogged all day long and then mending linen in the evening. I was underhousemaid and while there the kitchen maid, who was very fat, had been to a Fairground and on her return home to bed was groaning all night with pain. In the night my bed was removed to the head housemaid's room. I was a poor ignorant little thing and hadn't a clue what was on. Anyway the doctor was called in the morning and the girl had to go

---

[109] a jelly or blanc-mange moulded into ornamental shape : OED

home. Before a taxi was called I nipped in to say goodbye and meekly asked what the doctor had said. She replied "he says I have a lump in my inside, no business to be there." Off she went and when I went in to lunch at the Servants' Hall they all asked me in chorus what Alice said. I repeated her story and they rocked their sides with laughter. The joke was on me alright.

Until a new kitchen maid arrived I had to help out and My God did I get in a flick.[110] What I remember most was the stock pot on the floor of the larder with two mice floating around in it and the cook most evenings letting me do the donkey work while she sat in the kitchen on her young man's knee. One way and the other I had to grow up pretty quickly. For all that I wouldn't wish my life any different except that my sisters take their share looking after father. It's a case of all work and no play making Jack a dull boy. If it were possible that we could all get together and go over old times we'd have a good laugh, I'll bet. To a certain extent there's nothing like having a large family for I'm sure our parents used to get a lot of fun out of us when we had a 'do', sitting up till the small hours drinking wine and cider and smoking endless cigarettes I expect. I feel sure that none of us lost anything by being in a big family except lack of education. I know families grown up who hang around home and get on each others nerves. Perhaps I may sound to the reader a bit contradictory after my miserable attitude at the beginning, wishing this and that, but all I wished was to go to Grammar School and justify myself to myself, and not feel such a failure. I often feel I haven't a friend in the world. Largely because I make myself very unpopular by having the courage of my own convictions. I was talking it over with my father recently and then somehow we got around to discussing religion and I do love the way I can converse with him and get quite a bit of comfort out of it. He asked me if I learned the Sankie and Moody[111] hymn "Dare to

---

[110] to be in a flutter (become agitated) : EDD
[111] hugely popular American hymn writers. Moody & Sankey toured England in 1873 and their books of hymns were widely used

be a Daniel" and of course I did and straight away sang it over and felt a lot better for it. I think that Hymn describes me pretty thoroughly. I am one of those people who stand alone in this taking care of my father and having the courage in spite of the opposition of my sisters and brother.

I always feel very sad over my father at Xmas time for he must worry about my having to split my time up so. For myself I couldn't care less as I love New Years Day best. It gives me a new feeling of new life, new hope, everything just beginning and I find after months of depression which I always find descends on me like a cloud when September comes (ever since my precious son was killed by a bomb at school)[112] I can square my shoulders up and make a fresh start. It's a grand feeling whether it snows, rains or blows. We, and when I say we I mean most of us, have forgotten the meaning of Christmas. I used to work for a gentleman once who on arrival at his office mornings would look around his staff and say, "If I was dictator I'd have you all beheaded." Not always he'd say it but quite often when he was in a bad mood. I'd like to say now that if I was a Dictator I'd abolish the Christmas present and Father Xmas lark. Its nothing but a nightmare to most people and what's called a tradesman's harvest. I'd say lets go back to the beginning and really learn and know the meaning of Christmas.

Lillian with her son George (killed at Petworth school) and her daughter Susan.

---

[112] Lillian's only son George was killed on 29th September, 1942 when a bomb hit Petworth School

I'll never forget the Christmas when I was quite a big school girl and children said there wasn't a Father Christmas and I just couldn't believe it. So I went home from Sunday School and asked my father for the truth. He said "Do you want the truth?" and I said "Yes". He admitted there was no such a person and I was very sadly disillusioned.

I'm glad tonight is my night off duty for it is New Years Eve and some times I can't take all my father's spooky stories just as we are off to bed. Last night I was there and he told me that if I went and sat in my Parish Church porch at midnight I'd see all the people go into church who would go in as corpses during the following year. I suppose he means I'd see them in ghost's form pass into the church. He is a very difficult person to understand for he always fidgets about his health a lot yet can sit and tell me spooky things like the above as calmly as you please. Sometimes it just washes over me but other times I could just scream.

I was telling him last night how my little grand daughter had fallen and hurt herself and I persuaded her Mummy to get the doctor and he said "You ought to have done what I did years ago. I'd tossed a piece of stone up into a Harvest plum tree to knock some off and some of the gals were there, mother gone out. I had my old Trilby Hat on and while the stone was in the air a bramble knocked it off and the sharp edged stone stuck into my head and made it bleed. I said "go in and find a big spiders web, Olive." And she did. I clapped it on my sore head then put my hat on and never had any more trouble."
He tells me in the old days spiders webs were used a lot to check bleeding, finest thing you could have he said. His father used to dab a nice clean piece of clay on a cut and it healed up alright.

People will be out and about in Pubs enjoying themselves tonight and it reminds me of a pub story that my father told me sometime ago about a man who used to stand up in a Pub and sing till people got sick of it for he hadn't much of a voice. One night he was up on his feet singing when somebody played a trick on him. He finished his song and picked up his hat, put it on and everybody looked horrified because blood streamed down his face. One chap said "Ban't hurt much be ye mate?" and then somebody laughed and on examination it was found to be red ink. That finished his song singing.

Once again I am caught up in superstition for when I was talking to my father about the New Year I said "It's supposed to be unlucky to wash on New Years Day." and he said "Yes I've read about it in the weekly you bring me." He says "You read it." and I do and it isn't very explanatory but I tell him my version heard a few years ago and it says "If you wash on New Years Day you wash someone away." Poor old boy his other daughter washes his clothes on Wednesdays and he says "I'll put it off till next week" and I weakly agreed for I don't wash on New Years Day. Just how silly can one get? But it's right in our systems and has been all down the years. I guess we are weird people.

When I tell him it was wrong to tell us these superstitions when children he has such a lovely way of wriggling out of it. I can't help laughing yet can't dismiss it. Shows a weak streak in my character. I'm afraid when you are brought up in it, it sticks to you like shit to a blanket; I've heard my father use that expression a good many times. I do believe I could fill a page with the different things which were supposed to bring bad luck:-

Unlucky to put a hand bill[113] on table
Unlucky to put new shoes on table
Unlucky to see New Moon through window
Unlucky to do things fresh on a Friday
Unlucky to pick up a flower someone has dropped
Unlucky to take flowers to a new house
Unlucky to spill salt
Unlucky to see white cats

---

[113] a sharp tool with a short handles used in cutting underwood etc : DSD

Unlucky to pick up a knife
Unlucky to see just one magpie
Unlucky when, having started out on a journey to come back
for something, without sitting down and crossing legs three
times
Unlucky to burn holly
and unlucky to bring it over the threshold before Xmas Eve

(my father just won't have it but my husband does it about a week
before to make Wreaths)

Unlucky to cut green Elder or burn it
Unlucky to wear green clothes

We were never allowed to bring May Blossom indoors and once since
living here I came home with arms full of flowering Broom when a
neighbour looked out of her window and said "That's awful unlucky".

Its considered unlucky to pass a person on the stairs
Its very unlucky to transplant Parsley
Its unlucky to bring Lily of the Valley indoors also snowdrops

My father heard a man say in a pub that he wouldn't take snowdrops
indoors if anybody offered him 5£. I don't know how I've survived all
these horrors, I'm sure.

Our latest superstition is that we keep our mistletoe all through the
Year, only throwing it away as we get some new! That is supposed to
keep you from want. It's very amusing for the last few years the only
thing which has kept my husband and I from want is no smokes, no
drinks, no holidays so where the mistletoe comes in I don't quite know.

I know a man who says its bad luck to carry one halfpenny about in
one's pocket. If he finds himself in that state he throws the ha'penny

away. The Xmas tree is a bug to bear with some folk too, for if you buy one and after Xmas plant it in your garden and it dies someone of the family is supposed to die before the year is out.

I'm more than amused about the white cats because a friend of mine hasn't visited Hampers Green since, on returning home with her up to Petworth over two years ago we saw two white cats sitting on a wall; although it was dark she could see them plainly and nearly went mad with hysteria saying "It's a bad omen". I calmed her down by telling her I have to pass them every night sitting on the banks by Bedham Manor. This friend is quite laughable really as in the days when I worked with her we used to air our superstitions to each other. She used to have a jolly good laugh with me and if I was fussy over certain superstitions she hadn't heard of she'd say "I'm not taking on any more, I've quite enough of my own."

We had a groom lodging with us who was terrified if he saw one magpie and, on one occasion he was having a meal in the kitchen just before leaving to catch a train home to Ireland. He looked out the window and there on a Plum tree sat a magpie and the perspiration broke out all over Paddy's face and he said "Jusus look at that Bloody bird. I'll never reach London never mind Ireland." But he did. I had to talk to him and tease him out of his jitters.

I've just remembered such an amusing story my father told me one day about 3 ladies who farmed Buckfold Farm and the young man who worked for them. They thought he was "no end of a fellah" for work. He was sent out into the fields to work very early and then called in to breakfast. Just before he went into the house he used to dip his head into a bucket of water on the well to make it look as though he'd bust himself with work. When he went in dripping wet they'd all exclaim "oh dear you mustn't work so hard and sweat like that, you'll catch a chill."

They worked hard themselves and were very careful with their money. They all wore large aprons with pockets also large so that they could collect chips of wood etc and so save other firing. One night thieves broke in and robbed the poor old dears of all they had.

My father when listening to the big Robberies on the Radio is always saying that it is no worse than it used to be for he can remember a Farmer or Smallholder I'll say, who lived years ago at Strood Green who had killed a pig and hung it up in the Scullery for the night. Thieves got in and took it and he vowed next time he killed a pig he'd stay up with his gun but the thieves came again the next time and although he was there with his gun he was afraid to shoot so they got away with it again.

My father also remembers being told how a large gang of poachers notified a large land owner of their intention to poach on his estate and they carried out their threat and had a midnight feast in the large grounds. They were very daring and would stop at nothing to get what they wanted. There was also a gang of poachers who used to poach a lot on another estate at Kirdford and a keeper shot at one of them as he waded through the river. He was fatally wounded but when dying he wouldn't give any of them away. The old Keeper hung himself in the end. One poacher was a woman and she carried their birds on a belt under her big skirt. She was caught but my father says they don't punish women poachers. She was taken to the big house and put before a big spread of food but she wouldn't eat or drink or speak and after some hours she was released.

I must mention that when my mother was alive and we'd all left home and married she used to love having a sleep on Sunday afternoons but father used to love having a wander rounds the woods and often he'd meet picnickers and have a gossip with them. One day a gentleman offered him a packet of cigarettes and he said "Thank you" and calmly put them in his pocket. I'm sure he was only meant to take one. When he told his family at a later date some laughed and his eldest son-in-law thought it pretty good for somebody who'd lived in the country all his life.

My mother's uncle used to make clothes pegs and she got my father on to it and many a dozen he made before he got ill two years ago. He used to make them beautifully and I and my sister used to find customers for them and he used to buy his tobacco with it, but now he doesn't smoke he won't try and make clothes pegs. He is a queer cuss for he now blames me that his washing wasn't done on New Years Day as he always blames me that he gave up smoking. He was also very clever at making birch brooms and doing other things with wood.

I miss terribly the days when he used to come through the wood to meet me on summer evenings, and collect his kindling wood. He always reminded me of the children's verse which goes like this:

> Mr. Weeman was a woodman who lived in Dingle dell,
> He had a little chopper and used it very well.

I don't know why old men always look so pathetic and melt my heart so much but they do.

I love some of father's sayings for when I tell him about some of our local builders who have sprung up the last few years he says they may get on alright but what if they fall on hard times, a trade slump or something? He says

> "larger boats can venture o'er,
> but little boats must stay on shore."

There is a lot of difference in people about being devoted to their sons, some boast how clever they are. He tells me there was a man who lived at Hilliers Lodge, Horsham Road whose son made a kind of windmill all beautifully carved out representing two men sawing wood with a crosscut saw. It was a lovely thing and people used to stand and stare at it and the old man used to look up at it and say "Ah you can look and you can stare but you can't do it an' I can't do it."

We were discussing names of copses one day and how my father remembers them I can't think or how they got their names. From the Fittleworth/Wisborough Green Road near Mockbeggars there's Blagdens Copse, Balcomes Copse, Holiday Copse, Holiday Rue and Shipfields Hanger and finally Tar Hanger. Working in copses is a very healthy life my father tells me, it's a good appetiser the smell of wood as well as the fresh air. It makes him very sad that we have to buy wood and when we get it he has to rely on me and my sister splitting it up. His old cottage is very smoke pickled and I don't notice it until I get back home and hang my raincoat up on the kitchen door and I get whiffs of it each time I brush past it.

My husband told my father recently how they'd been doing a job at Parham. "Coo" he says "when my father was a boy living at Cootham, the gentleman at Parham House was notorious for the queer things he did but at the same time he was very generous and had lots of food cooked for all the poor people on and around his place.[114] However trying he was nobody complained because he was so generous. One day a tramp went up to the kitchen door and asked for something to eat and drink and he was given food on the Master's orders and then the Master said "You asked for a drink" and he instructed the servants to stand him in a barrel of cider up to his neck and he said "Now you can drink as much as you like." Poor Tramp.

One day a young woman was walking through the park with a basket of butter which she had to deliver somewhere for sale and it may have

---

[114] the Hon Robert Curzon (1774-1863) and his son Robert later 14th Lord Zouche (1810-1873) would have been at Parham House when George Elliott Snr. was a boy in the 1840's

81

been to the big house but anyway the Master met her in the Park and he asked her what she'd got. When she told him he told her to turn round and pull up her clothes right over her head and the next thing he did was to throw all the packets of butter at her B.T.M,[115] after which he paid for the butter and told her to take it back home and do what she liked with it.

The same gentleman hated people to collect chestnuts from his park and having put a man on guard, he dressed up like a tramp and went out and collected chestnuts. The man on guard told him he wasn't allowed to do it but the tramp ignored him and went on collecting them so the guard said "If you don't stop it I'll give you a good hidin'." He, the tramp, went on picking up chestnuts till the guard gave him a good thrashing till he squealed and then admitted who he was. The guard said "Serves ye right, I did as I was told."

Somewhere out that way a man had a beloved pony and when it died he had him buried with all his harness which he called his "regimentals".

While thinking about these weird people doing things, a man according to my father was looking for a plant called "break stone parsley"[116] and it was supposed to be, when scalded, a cure for gravel bladder trouble. One day he came upon a poor old man breaking stones beside the road (I myself can just remember the lumps of stone beside the road to Petworth). Anyway this man said "Can you tell me where I can find some break stone parsley?" and the old man was deaf and he said "Break stones faster be buggered, doin' it fast enough now."[117]

When my precious grandchild Amanda was breaking up for the Xmas holiday she returned from her school at Midhurst at 12 o'clock. She

---

[115] a polite slang expression for bottom or bum. JG
[116] possibly pepper saxifrage
[117] the old man may have been George Elliott Snr as in old age he worked on the roads as a stone breaker

was 8 years and a bit absent minded like her grandmother, and was told several times to wait for me on my return to Petworth from Bedham. Poor wee thing had to wait 10 minutes and got very cold and anxious but eventually Nanny, as she calls me, arrived and we did our shopping before leaving for Hampers Green. Amanda by then was almost in tears with cold but as we got to North Street I saw a man I hadn't seen for years who used to work in Petworth. I greeted him by saying "Hallo stranger" and he answered me in much the same strain. Having got by Amanda said "who is that Nanny?" and I said "Mr. Yallop". She thought it a very funny name and immediately it reminded me of a story my father told me. Now when his mother was a girl, boys were employed by farmers to walk round and round their corn fields singing the following ditty as loud as they could

> Ey all up, Ey all up,
> Yer pickin' the master's corn.
> Tis but a liddle
> And that's in the middle,
> Ey all up, Ey all up

These boys were paid the large sum of 2d. per day. I sang it over to Amanda and her tears dried up at once and we hummed it over all the way home which cheered her up no end.[118] I love the way children can change from tears to smiles like a rainbow after a shower. It's a wonderful thing to my mind. I often watch my little grandson after a tumble, how he picks himself up and the smile breaks through the big tears on his fat little cheeks.

This morning on the Radio we heard about the trouble in Cyprus and my father and I talk about the British Troops out there and some other place as well. He says, "No difference than when I was a boy for two

---

[118] Lillian's Grandmother 'was a girl' in the early 1840's. Lillian and her Granddaughter Amanda were singing a 'ditty' handed down over 4 generations and at least 120 years.

of my cousins went to the Afghan War[119] and one was injured by a
poisonous arrow and always had a running wound on his jaw." The
brother could never take intoxicating liquours, just one drink would
make him queer. My father says they were in a jungle and never saw
their enemies. They were glad to get back home he says.

This is Saturday night and I've been at my father's all day, working
very hard getting cleaning done and running a fresh load of cut wood
into the shed with my truck.[120] I do enjoy Saturdays when I can stay at
Bedham, it gives me a break from doing both homes. Also I can relax
in the evening and listen to my father's talk of days gone by which
he loves relating to me. He has just told me a story about an oldish
couple who were hoeing turnips for a farmer. They sat under a hedge
having just boiled up their billy can of tea and taken the lid off to cool.
Presently the man said,
"It's rainin' Dame."
"No" says she,
"Well" he said, "it's just started, for I saw it when it dropped into our
billy can."
When they looked up a boy sat up in a tree and was tiddling down into
their tea can. There used to be plenty of naughty boys about even in
those days you see.

Still they had to work very hard and must have got very tired and fed
up. My father tells me of a boy who had to work with a team of horses
ploughing and when they went up the field and back they called it a
"bout"[121]. One day the boy, who was living in the farmhouse, was
working with his Master and it was pancake day and he couldn't wait
for night and a feed but Master kept saying "just one more 'bout'

---

[119] The Second Anglo Afghan War 1878 - 80
[120] A handcart, Lillian was not able to drive.
[121] In Sussex dialect a 'bout' is a day's work (DSD) however in this context it
is short for 'to turn about' as in to go up the field and back then 'turn about'
and go back again : JG

84

and then" and the boy said "What then, Master?" and he said "then another" and the boy thought it was dreadful. Still eventually Master packed up and they went in to tea after feeding the horses, and the boy was thrilled when he had his first pancake and he said to Master "That's one pancake." And the Master said "What then?" And the boy got his own back by saying "then another" and so on. The farmer thoroughly enjoyed it or it wouldn't be remembered and talked about.

One year my father went to Angmering near Littlehampton harvesting and they stayed in a lonely barn the first night and it so happened that Littlehampton was celebrating and he said he saw the firework display which was a wonderful sight from where they were, he wouldn't wish to be closer. They could see King George the 5th in fireworks and all sorts of things. He didn't like the lonely barn so asked the farmer if he could doss nearer the farm and he said "Oh yes, you can sleep in the Root house if you like." So this he and his mate did. Next morning a man came and peeped in at them, one of the workers, and they got talking and he asked where they came from and my father said "Bedham".
"Well" he said "I married my wife from Bedham. It was a cottage with a long path of flag stones down to the door."
"Well that's where I live," said my Father.
This man's name was Roberts and he married a woman named Sebbage.[122] This man worked for 50 years on the same farm at Angmering and at the end of that time he was working one day and the boss said "You'd better have a day off, here's a 1£ note, go out for a holiday." Mr. Roberts was so lost that he just hung around the garden all day. Just a bit different from the present day and all the dissatisfaction and strikes. Makes one feel very ashamed. I often am

---

[122] Census returns and Parish Registers for Angmering and Fittleworth show that Fredrick Roberts of Old Place Farm, Angmering married Mary Sebbage of Bedham. Mary died in 1869 aged 39 and some years later Mr. Roberts remarried.

when I listen to the stories of demands for more money all the time. It'll be the ruination of our Islands I'm afraid.

Thinking about staying in the garden a man had a bit of ground which was very rough and he wanted it dug up quickly so he had a bash at it himself – and then adjourned to a pub and while in there he whispered to a chap and showed him a sovereign covered in mud. The next night he went along to the pub again and this time he had two sovereigns covered in mud. He said "Don't say nothin' about it will ye." Next night he had three so the chaps in the pub all got to know it and after he'd gone home they took lanterns to this bit of ground and dug like mad until the ground was all turned over but never a thing did they find. Very clever I must say. My father swears its true but I wonder.

Like the story of the body snatchers which really is true for his mother had told him about it and the body snatchers took their bodies to a man named Dr. Mud[123] and he'd give them 10/- for the body. One night the men felt pretty desperate because they hadn't got one and they wanted the money ever so badly. They talked it over and the smallest man consented to getting into a sack and being taken to the Doctor's house. So off they went and when they got to his surgery he was very busy and he just glanced at the sack and said in an undertone "Just pop it into the cellar, I'll see to it presently." He gave them 10/- and they carted their mate down the cellar and left him to it. Late that night the Doctor went to the cellar and opened the sack and out crawled a live man. Did the Doctor curse and swear and he said "You can go but I'll have you yet." But he never did.

Thinking about mean tricks my father was once at the Fox pub when he was a lad. He had been to a court case with some local people about some hoop making and they had got very hungry so they bought some sausages at Petworth and returned to the Fox Pub where the landlady allowed them to fry them. It was also a shop and they bought bread

---

[123] See Appendix 5 Body Snatching

etc and all settled themselves ready for a feast. A man and sons and daughter were already there who had a caravan down the road. Sort of a conjuring party and while the sausages were cooking somebody started a fight outside and everybody rushed out to have a look. George and the girl were the only ones left in the room and George (my father) went to the window to look out and when he turned his back the girl from the conjuring party had collared up the frying pan with the 2lb of sausages and bolted off. The fighting died out and they all got done out of their meal. My father was too young to deal with them he says but I can't think how they let them get away with it.

A farmer went to a fair and sale at a place a few miles from this district and he had a look round at the ponies and horses just for the sake of it, because he didn't want one. While doing so a chap came up to him with a collar on like a parson and said "I think that's a jolly good pony and if I could only stay for the sale I'd bid 20£, but I can't stay now." "Well" the farmer said "I don't mind biddin' for the pony if you're coming back before the sale is over."
And the parson assured him he would. The farmer bid the 20£ but never saw the so called parson any more. He (the parson) was the bloke who wanted to flog the pony and did it very well. The farmer was properly had poor chap.

Another young man went down to Arundel with his father's pony and a chap came up to him and said "You've got a lovely pony there, come and have a drink." He did, when he came outside his pony was gone and he never saw it anymore.

Another farmer went to the local sale and sold his horse which he used in the trap to go about in then went into a pub and had a few drinks. They came out and looked around for another horse to drive back home with. He had a mate with him and they saw a horse they took a fancy to and looked him over and paid for him. When they put the horse in the trap the farmer said "You'd really think he knows which way he's goin' sims re'lar 'tome in the shafts." And off they went home. Next morning his old horse looked out of the stable with the star on his forehead which had been painted over. Just shows what a few drinks will do to a man, don't it.

This morning at Bedham I had a great thrill. I am a great bird lover and always feed them a lot, chasing the big Jays away when I feel they have more than their share. On my way to the lavatory, which I must point out is, as it always has been, under the yew tree a distance from the house, all the small birds followed me twittering very loudly. Then when I left there I went up the garden where on a clothes post I have a thermometer which gives my father great pleasure. The birds followed me up there and I told them they must wait until father and I had breakfast. When I returned to the house I told my father about them and he said "That's nothin' when I was a young man and worked for a time at Upperton Village I used to go through the Park by the Kennels and there I'd see an old woman feeding magpies and they perched on her head and shoulders etc. You could hardly see her for magpies."

Another woman at Oldham Hill used to be seen with one perched on her head and people thought she was a witch. I've a way to go before I come into that category. But if I ever had to live alone that would be one of my favourite hobbies, to make friends with the little feathered friends. I love watching the Rabbits getting up in the morning in the poor old derelict garden which I haven't the strength to cultivate.

It is Sunday morning, I am just off to collect my father's bundle of kindling wood. When we were children we were never allowed to fetch wood on Sundays being told "You see that man up in the moon with a faggot up to his back, well he was sent there because he collected wood on Sunday mornings."

I never hear my father say that now because he is only too anxious to have the wood.

We had to be very good on Sundays as children, walking to Fittleworth to Sunday School as I may have mentioned before. So if a very witchy looking old lady is to be seen up in the moon with a bundle of wood on her back and a bright blue "Bushman" saw in her hand, that will be me. Perhaps we could start up a new life on the moon and get things ready for the many people below who are trying to get there. My precious only daughter loves saying to me when I get back to Hampers and she calls on me "You're not with it Mum." and I say "Of course I'm not, I'm still up in the woods at Bedham with the witches and the birds that I love.

I love watching the expressions on people's faces when I step out of the bus at Petworth, some speak and some hurry past that weird looking creature with muddy Wellingtons on and hair all askew with earrings on. The poor old "Fuddy Duddy" chuckles to herself and thinks the people who hurry past me don't know what they are missing. I love the mud and the trees. I love staring at the beautiful trees as we go up round Hairpin bend with the headlights on them and the rabbits hopping out of the way, its really lovely.

I have done my best to Honour my Father and my Mother and shall continue to do so. I always hope and pray I will be given the strength to do it but often feel in my bones that fate in some way will take a hand. Maybe it's because a few years ago my doctor and also my father's doctor told me my father will still be sitting in his chimney corner when I've worn myself out with the effort. I have, on looking back over my life, always been the one to do things for my father. I remember when I was a child going out with a storm lantern to Arundel Holt woods to meet him and he said "Whatever made you come to look for me?' I also stayed up far into the night after mother and the rest had gone to bed, keeping him company while he mended all our boots. I often had great difficulty to keep awake. Sometimes I'd read the West Sussex Gazette to him.

God bless him, and I hope he'll live to be a hundred and I'll still be waiting on him. He who lives longest will see most…

- - - - - -

George Elliott lived to 103. He stayed in his beloved cottage at
Bedham until he was 93 then, after a short spell in the Petworth
Cottage Hospital, he went to live with Lillian and her husband Charlie
at Hampers Green.   He died 9 years later.

Lillian died in 1998, she was 92. Her husband Charlie died in 1995.

It was always her wish to write and have her work published. To know
that the stories that the Whitington and Elliott families had so faithfully
handed down over so many years, and that she had lovingly collected
and recorded, were being read and enjoyed by others who love the
countryside, its history and traditions as much as she did would, in her
words, have been for her "a great thrill".

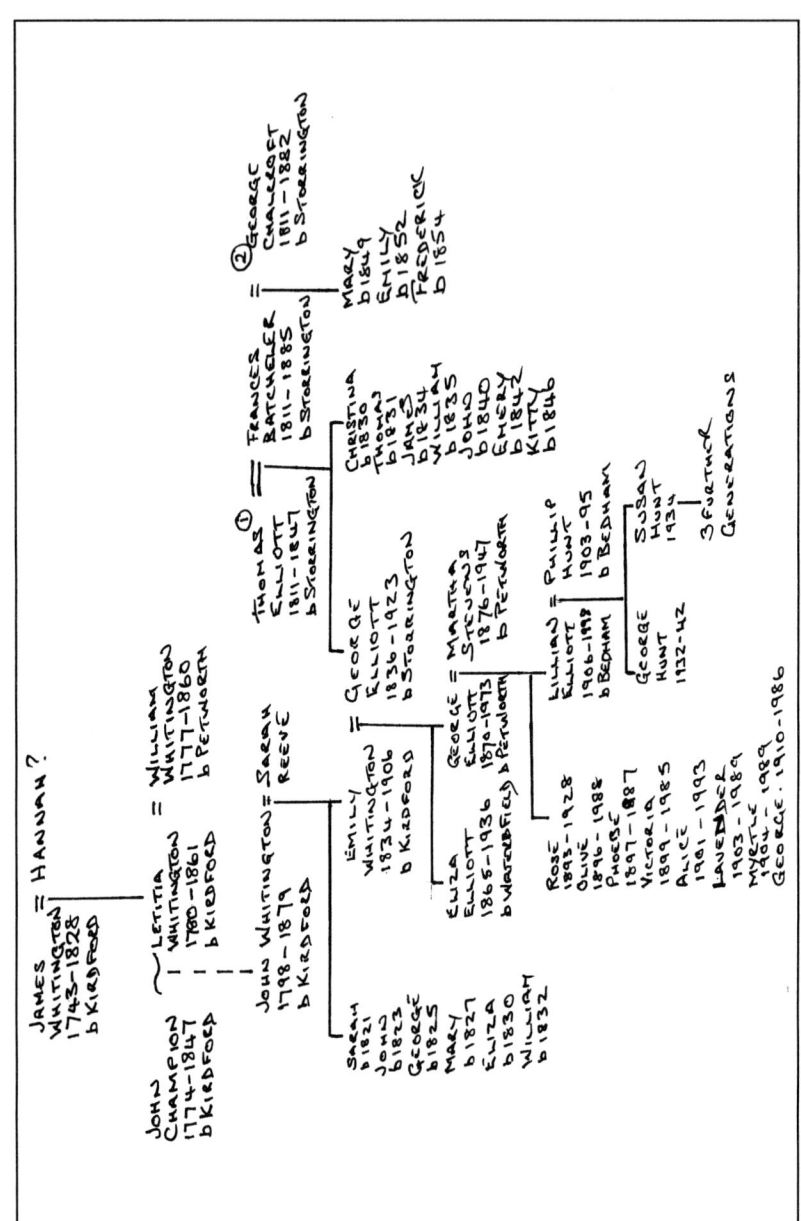

The Whitington & Elliott Family Tree.

92

Appendix 1 - The Whitingtons & the Elliotts

The Whitington's were a long established family of Agricultural Labourers living in Kirdford and the surrounding parishes. Research carried out to date shows that the family were certainly in the area from 1700 and may well extend back further generations.

Although she was proud of her Elliott heritage Lillian was quite clear that the stories her father told her "had been handed down from one generation to another by Whitingtons". The earliest story in Lillian's manuscript that it has been possible to verify and date conclusively occurred in 1735. This story was recounted to Lillian by her father in the mid 1960's and his account was substantially accurate. (See Appendix 4) At the time of it's telling this story had been passed down through six successive generations of the family. The Whitington family is quite remarkable not just for the length of their oral tradition but because the information is passed on with an astonishing degree of factual accuracy.

The first of the Whitington's to be named in Lillian's account is her great great great grandfather James Whitington born in 1743, although at least one of the stories has clearly been handed down from an earlier generation. In 1798 James' 18 year old daughter Letitia had an illegitimate son, John Whitington, the father was John Champion (See Appendix 2). Four years later Letitia married William Whitington of Petworth and the couple set up home at Strood Green. Although this line has not yet been fully traced William and Letitia had at least three children and lived at Strood Green until their deaths in 1860 & 1861 respectively.

At some time probably before 1820 John Whitington (Lillian's great grandfather) moved to the Storrington area to work. After an accident in which he broke his leg he moved back to Kirdford and in June 1821 married Sarah Reeve of Wisborough Green. The couple had seven children, all of whom were born at Kirdford. The youngest of these, Emily, was Lillian's grandmother.

Sometime between the end of 1834 and 1841 the family moved to Sullington Lane Cottage, Sullington and it was here that the Whitington children grew up. The family later moved to Springhead near Parham, although by this time Emily was the only one of the children still living at home. They then moved to Watersfield.

On 30th May, 1863 Emily Whitington married George Charles Elliott at Coldwaltham Church. Their first child, Eliza was born at Watersfield in 1865. Shortly after this the couple moved to Little Wickers, just outside Petworth, it was here that their second surviving child George (Lillian's father) was born. Family accounts suggest that, late in her pregnancy, Emily suffered a bad fall while collecting water from the dipping hole near Wickers, this resulted in a very difficult birth. The repercussions of this difficult birth meant that Emily was, for the rest of her life, 'frail'. Despite this she worked consistently, initially in various casual agricultural jobs and, towards the end of her life as a Charwoman.

In 1871 Emily's mother Sarah died and her father moved in with his daughter and her family. At the end of 1874 the family moved to Mants Cottage, Bedham and it was there in 1879 that John Whitington died, close to his boyhood home and many of his Whitington relatives.

It would appear that family relationships among the Whitington's were close. Although John Whitington and his family had moved away from Kirdford and he and his wife were illiterate, links were maintained with his mother and stepfather at Strood Green. The 1851 Census shows Emily and her mother Sarah visiting Letitia and her family and so when Emily and her family moved to Petworth and then to Bedham she would certainly have known her relatives in the area.

Although Emily herself could not write, she in turn maintained close links with her brothers and sisters. Her brother William had moved to Westbury-on-Severn and correspondence among Lillian's papers show that Emily remained in touch with him and even arranged for her son George to spend time with his uncle.

The Elliott's also have a long history in Sussex. As they are not the central storytellers in this account their line has not been traced to the same extent as the Whitingtons. However from the Parish Records of Storrington, Parham Archives and other sources it is clear that the Elliotts had been living and working on the farms in and around Storrington for at least as long as the Whitingtons had been in the Kirdford area.

George Elliott Senior (Lillian's paternal grandfather) was born at Cootham, just outside Storrington, and it was here, particularly around Brick Common, that his branch of the Elliott family was centred. George's father Thomas Elliott, an Agricultural Labourer married Frances Batchelor, daughter of Charles Batchelor, a tailor from Storrington, and his wife Abby.

Thomas and Frances Elliott (Lillian's paternal great grandparents) had nine children, two of whom died in infancy. Their last child, Kitty was born in 1846 and a few months later in February 1847 Thomas died. Although two of the children had left home Frances was left with five young children, in May of the following year she married George Chalcroft, an Agricultural Labourer also of Storrington. They had three children.

George Elliott lived with his mother and step-father at Cootham until the early 1860's when he moved to Coldwaltham. Shortly afterwards he married Emily Whitington.

Unlike his wife George was literate. Although his mother Frances had not been to school it may well be that she was keen for all her children to receive an education. Her brothers were certainly literate and all her children, including the girls, went to school.

Appendix 2 - 'Come-by-chance' and the fight in the copse

Lillian's Great Grandfather John Whitington was indeed a 'come-by-chance' as she relates. Among the Poor Law Records for Kirdford is a Bastardy Bond which shows that on the 6th May 1798 Letty Whitington 'was delivered of a Male Bastard Child, at the House of her Father James Whitington in the said Parish of Kirdford'.

The Bond reveals that after questioning by George O'Brien Earl of Egremont and John Sargent Esquire, 'two of his Majesty's Justices of the Peace' 'John Champion the Younger' a Carpenter also of Kirdford was 'adjudged' to be the father of Letty's child. He was ordered to pay the Overseers of the Poor 'the Sum of Two Shillings Weekly and every Week...' towards 'Keeping, Sustentation and Maintenance' for as long as the child was 'chargeable to the said Parish'. On 19th February of the same year John Champion married Mary Hews also of Kirdford.

Illegitimate children under the age of seven who were the subject Bastardy Bonds of this type often remained with their mothers. However on reaching the age of seven children could be sent to work, either in the parish or to an employer outside the parish. In this case it would appear that John Champion had financial responsibility for his son John Whitington. It is therefore perfectly possible that when John reached the age of seven his father did come to claim him as described with the intention of sending him away to work.

When Lillian's father George was a boy his grandfather John Whitington lived with the family at Bedham. As Lillian says her 'father was really educated' by his grandfather, it is highly likely that he told his grandson about this dramatic incident in his boyhood. If the fight occurred as described, and there is no reason to suppose that it did not, James Whitington would have been 62 when, in 1805, he fought to keep his grandson. His opponent, John Champion, would have been 31.

Appendix 3 – John Whitington and a broken leg

Lillian relates how, when her great grandfather John Whitington was "working out under the downs he broke his leg", and had to return to Kirdford as "in those days they were taken back to the Parish where they were born and brought up." It is likely that John Whitington's accident occurred sometime before 1834 when what was known as the Old Poor Law was replaced by the Poor Law Amendment Act.

Under the Old Poor Law each individual had to have a place of Settlement, usually the parish in which they had been 'born and brought up', although there were other means of qualifying for settlement. It was the responsibility of the place of settlement to provide welfare assistance if a person was unable to earn their own living. If an individual was living away from their place of settlement and became destitute, the parish in which he or she was living at the time had the right to remove the pauper to his or her original place of settlement (or receive payment from it).

The story does not suggest that John's family were 'removed' with him, which they undoubtedly would have been had he been married with a family. It is likely then that the accident happened before 1821 when John was single and at the time he was probably a 'living in' labourer on one of the farms around Storrington.

Lillian says that he "had a dreadful journey" back to Kirdford; it is brief glimpse of an incident in the life of an otherwise fit young man. In describing her great grandfather's experience Lillian gives a sharp insight into what happened to people who moved away from home and found themselves without work. Under this system people of all ages, and often whole families, could be 'removed'.

Appendix 4 – Pressing or Peine forte et dure

The story that George Elliott told Lillian and her husband in the 1960s was told to him by his Grandfather Whitington and relates to an actual murder that took place at Little Bognor near Fittleworth in May 1735. The story must therefore have come originally from Lillian's great great great great grandfather. When George Elliott passed the story on to his daughter 230 years later the information that he passed on was substantially correct.

In May 1735 three men and a boy robbed a cottage at Little Bognor Common and murdered the occupant Elizabeth Symonds. Later the boy turned King's Evidence and two of the men were convicted and hanged at Horsham. The third man, John Weekes of Fittleworth refused to speak, remaining silent throughout his imprisonment and trial. Witnesses did come forward to testify that he was able to speak but he remained mute. At this time refusing to speak at your trial was an offence and John Weekes was "found guilty of standing mute through malice", the punishment for this was 'Peine forte et dure' or as it was more commonly know 'pressing'. John Weekes was therefore 'pressed' for the crime of refusing to plead to the charge of robbery and murder, not the actual crime itself.

By 1735 'peine forte et dure' was extremely rare in England. Despite the rarity of this sentence there were certain widely held beliefs associated with it, one of these being that if you remained silent at your trial your possessions were not forfeited to the Crown. This was not in fact true and at the trial the Judge, in trying to persuade John Weekes to speak, went to great lengths to explain this.

There were strict procedures governing how pressing should be carried out. These clearly state that:
the prisoner shall be sent to the prison from whence he came, and put into a mean room stopped from light...

the procedures then specify how the prisoner should be laid out and the progressive increasing of iron or stone weights. Unlike hanging, pressing was carried out away from the public gaze.

In Horsham however the rules were not followed. The pressing took place in the prison yard and a huge crowd gathered to watch. A witness described the scene

"a board of one hundredweight upon it, then one hundredweight more, and then a third hundredweight was added, but during all he remained mute. Fifty pounds more were added, when he appeared in the agonies of death; finally, the gaoler, who weighed over sixteen stone, laid himself in addition to the weights upon the board and killed the man instantly."

The use of this punishment with the further horror of it being carried out in public caused widespread shock and it was not used again in England.

Members of the Whitington family lived in Fittleworth and may well have known John Weekes. The Kirdford Whitingtons would certainly have known all about the crime, the trial and the punishment. Living so close to Horsham they probably knew people who had been present in the prison yard. Public hangings attracted big crowds, an exceptional event like this would have attracted crowds from all over the area and it may well be that some members of the family were present.

Appendix 5 – Body Snatching

In the early part of the 19th Century there was widespread public
concern over the activities of body snatchers, or resurrectionists as
they were often known, who dug up freshly buried corpses and sold
them for dissection. The Anatomy Act of 1832 was designed to curb
the illicit acquiring of bodies for sale and restrict dissection to licenced
practitioners, usually medical schools.

At first sight then it would appear that this story describes events before
1832. However this horrible activity may actually have been taking
place in Storrington as late as the 1850's or 1860's. The 1861 Census
for Storrington shows that at some time after 1851 Dr. Barrington
Mudd moved to the town and set up a medical practice in West Street,
he was accompanied by his brother Francis Mudd, a surgeon. The
Mudds came from Suffolk and had trained in Edinburgh.

Lillian says "like the story of the body snatchers which really is true
for his mother had told him'. In 1861 when Dr. Mudd and his brother
were living in West Street, Lillian's grandmother Emily Whitington, the
source of the story, was living nearby on the outskirts of Storrington!

The story suggests that this was not the first time the men had taken
bodies "to the Doctor's house", if this was the case it is no wonder the
doctor could only "curse and swear" as, if the story "really is true",
both the men and Dr. Mudd were engaged in a highly illegal activity.

By 1865 Emily Whitington had moved from Storrington. Francis
Mudd the surgeon died in 1866, aged 45. His brother Barrington Mudd
died in 1897, aged 74.

Lillian Mary Hunt, nee Elliott
1906 - 1998

Lillian Hunt was born at Bedham, in the Parish of Fittleworth, West Sussex in 1906, the eighth daughter in a family of eight girls and one boy. Her family had lived and worked in the area at least since 1700.

Throughout her life Lillian loved reading and writing and began to keep diaries and make notes, particularly of the local stories that she heard from her father and grandfather. In the 1960's she began to put these stories together, hoping to have them published. However her hectic life caring for her father and her husband and helping with her grandchildren, while at the same time working and running her home, meant that she did not have time to see her project through to publication.

Lillian's maternal grandmother was a Whitington from Kirdford. The Whitington's had a great oral tradition and it is down this line of the family that the majority of the stories have come. James Whitington passing them to his daughter Letitia and his grandson John. John in turn passed them to his daughter Emily (Lillian's grandmother). Emily passed them to her son George Elliott who, as he in turn passed them on, captured the imagination of his daughter Lillian. Lillian intended her book to be a tribute to her father and his life and her decision to title it 'Honour Thy Father' reflects this.

While it is a tribute to both her parents, it is also a tribute to Lillian herself. A remarkable lady from a remarkable family who, despite being only the second generation of that family able to read and write, recognized the importance of their oral tradition and between all her other tasks snatched moments to write it down.

Without her foresight and determination we would not such a marvellous insight into rural life in the 18th, 19th and early 20th centuries.

Bibliography

Albery, W., *A Millennium of Facts in the History of Horsham & Sussex, 947 – 1947* (Brighton: The Southern Publishing Co. Ltd., 1947)

Brodie, F.J., *The Great Drought of 1893*. (Q.J. Royal Meterol: Soc 20, 1-30, 1894)

Burchfield, R. W., (ed) *A Supplement to the Oxford English Dictionary*, (London: Oxford University Press, 1972)

Course. E., *The Railways of Southern England: Secondary & Branch Lines* (London: BT Batsford Ltd.,1974)

Dallaway, J., *The Parochial Topography of the Rape of Arundel in the Western Division of the County of Sussex Vol II*, (London: Bowyer, Nichols & Sons, 1831)

Evans, I .H., (ed) *Brewer's Dictionary of Phrase & Fable*, (London: Cassell, 1974)

------- *Field Guide to the Wild Flowers of Britain* (London: The Reader's Digest Association, 1981)

Parish, W.D., *A Dictionary of the Sussex Dialect & Collection of Provincialisms in use in the County of Sussex*, (Bexhill: Gardner's of Bexhill Ltd., 1957)

Step, E., *Wild Flowers Month by Month in Their Natural Haunts*, (London: The Westminster Gazette)

------- *The Oxford English Dictionary*, (London: Oxford University Press, 1970)

Tittensor, R.M., *A History of the Mens: A Sussex Woodland Common* (SAC 116 347-374, 1978)

Porter, N., (ed) *Dr. Webster's Unabridged Dictionary* (London: Bell & Daldy, 1864)

Wright, J., (ed) *The English Dialect Dictionary* (London: Oxford University Press, 1961)

Abbreviations

DSD   Dictionary of Sussex Dialect

EDD   English Dialect Dictionary

JG   Jennifer Goldsmith

OED   Oxford English Dictionary